SHADES OF GREY
GLASGOW 1956-1987

SHADES
OF GREY

GLASGOW 1956-1987

Photographs by

OSCAR
MARZAROLI

Words by

WILLIAM
McILVANNEY

Notes from
JOE FISHER *and* CORDELIA OLIVER

MAINSTREAM
PUBLISHING
in conjunction with

THIRD EYE CENTRE
350 Sauchiehall St., Glasgow G2 3JD

First published in Great Britain in 1987 by
MAINSTREAM PUBLISHING COMPANY (EDINBURGH) LTD
7 Albany Street,
Edinburgh EH1 3UG,
in conjunction with
THIRD EYE CENTRE (GLASGOW) LTD

ISBN 1 85158 047 6 (cloth)

British Library Cataloguing in Publication Data
Marzaroli, Oscar
Glasgow 1956-87: shades of grey . . . . .
1. Glasgow (Strathclyde) — History
I. Title II. McIlvanney, William
941.4'43085   DA890.G5

ISBN 1-85158-047-6

Typeset in Garamond by EUSPB, 48 Pleasance, Edinburgh EH8 9TJ

Printed in Great Britain by Butler & Tanner Ltd, Frome

Photograph selection and layout: Christopher Carrell (Third Eye Centre)
and Oscar Marzaroli

Design and finished artwork: James Hutcheson and Paul Keir

Third Eye Centre is financially assisted by the Scottish Arts Council
and Glasgow District Council

CONTENTS

ACKNOWLEDGEMENTS

As well as pursuing his own interests as a photographer, Ken Murray has been Oscar Marzaroli's darkroom technician since 1982, and in this capacity has produced thousands of fine prints for exhibition, publication and for sale. Frequently working under considerable pressure, his darkroom quality and dedication have always been of the highest standard.

Anne Marzaroli has been an unfailing source of advice and support throughout the long preparation of this book. She remained patient and objective even during the most frantic and chaotic periods of production, and a considerable debt is owed to her.

Thanks are also due to the Marzaroli daughters, Marie-Claire, Nicola, Lisa-Jane, and their friends Martin Maccabe and Derek Stuart who helped in many different and invaluable ways.

Joe Fisher and Cordelia Oliver have worked with considerable diligence and great patience in the time-consuming task of compiling the notes to the photographs, and responding to our many queries. Joe Fisher's involvement with the publication began at an early stage, and he has always been extremely generous with both his time and his extensive knowledge of Glasgow.

Finally, as this publication has emerged from two major exhibitions, and one previous publication, thanks are due to the staff of Third Eye Centre for their commitment to, and belief in, Oscar Marzaroli's work.

PREFACE

Third Eye Centre's association with Oscar Marzaroli began with his agreement to have a number of his photographs included in "Noise and Smoky Breath", a collection of poems and visual images of Glasgow from 1900 to 1983, first published in May 1983. My first visit to his studio was a memorable one, seeing the full range of Marzaroli's work unfold, spanning as it does, over thirty years. In subject matter it covers much of Scotland, particularly the Highlands and Islands, and the Arts, as well as Glasgow.

From this initial visit and selection of images, a relationship developed which has subsequently encompassed two major Third Eye Centre exhibitions — "One Man's World: Photographs 1955-84" (April 1984), with an accompanying monograph, and "Shades of Grey: Photographs of Glasgow 1956-1986" (December 1986).

It is the Glasgow photographs on which Marzaroli's reputation will ultimately rest. As George Oliver commented in his Introduction to "One Man's World", "Marzaroli's view of Glasgow can bear comparison, I believe, with other important photographers' views of their favoured places: with Andreas Feininger's pictures of Chicago and New York, for example: with the Paris seen by Fritz Henle and Brassai; or the British Isles seen through the eyes and camera of the sensitive Edwin Smith . . . no other photographer, to my knowledge, has caught the look and the life of Glasgow with comparable accuracy and sympathy. . . . He has, too, such a highly developed eye for the most effective picture; for precision and accuracy of placing within its borders; for mood — and with Glasgow's particular climatic fickleness, mood is never too far away: soft or hard or somewhere in between. He is acutely sensitive to subtleties of light and with his highly professional mastery of technical method well able to record it all in the final print."

The three hundred photographs reproduced in this book have been chosen from well over forty thousand. The selection has been determined primarily by the strength of the individual image, but it was also important to tell the story of the city and its people as witnessed and recorded by Marzaroli as fully as possible. Therefore a number of photographs have been chosen because of the information they give, and the contribution they make to this story. However, Marzaroli's involvement with the city has never been a self-conscious one, neither has he deliberately set out to systematically and comprehensively document the fabric and life of the entire city and its outlying areas. As an artist and compassionate observer, he has been drawn to certain subjects, particular areas, specific events and happenings. Chance as well as intent has played its part in determining which aspects of the city and its people engaged his attention. Marzaroli's involvement in Glasgow has been more active in some years and less so in others, as his revenue-producing work, mainly in film, dictated.

Given, therefore, the uneven nature of the record and the need to give it coherence and pattern in book form, we decided to establish a sequential framework within which to place the photographs. The images were grouped in associated subject categories, beginning with "Cityscapes" and ending with "New Glasgow". We have attempted by sympathetic placing of the subject groups to establish a loose but coherent narrative, one that comes naturally and honestly from the photographer's vision, approach and working method.

Inevitably some groups are more comprehensive than others, and in one or two instances several disparate subjects have been grouped together under a composite title. Within each section, where appropriate, chronological comparisons between "old" and "new" are made.

The Gorbals section is one of the strongest and most complete and Marzaroli sees his record of the changes that occurred during the 1960s as a microcosm of what has happened within the city at large.

Glasgow, since 1956, the date of the first photograph in this collection, has changed dramatically. Many of the images commemorate a city, a cityscape, and a way of life that has vanished forever. In the clamour of praise for the "new" Glasgow, and what has been achieved in the last decade, there is a danger that much of the "old", particularly those aspects considered less salubrious, will be censored and where possible quietly forgotten. For example, numerous approaches were made to the business sector in the hope that this publication would attract sufficient sponsorship to ensure the highest possible quality of reproduction. Invariably the reaction was that the view given of Glasgow was too depressing, that this was a past that Glasgow was attempting to move away from. A Marzaroli colour plate book promoting the "new" city was suggested instead!

The success of Marzaroli's Glasgow exhibition at Third Eye Centre, the current popular triumph of Tony Roper's "The Steamie", the sell-out audiences for the recent revival of "The Gorbals Story", the burgeoning "Glasgow Book" industry, all indicate a profound appreciation of, and interest in, the "old" Glasgow, and the sense of place and richness of community it increasingly personifies. It can be argued that the changes and achievements of the "new" Glasgow, garlanded with the nomination of European City of Culture 1990, can only be truly understood, appreciated and made effective in the light of the "old". The fabric of the city, as well as employment and leisure patterns, may be changing; its people, however, by and large, remain the same and, as William McIlvanney emphatically asserts in the concluding line of his essay, "Glasgow belongs to them".

In his photographs, Marzaroli has caught the look and the heart of Glasgow — the old and the new, and he celebrates both. As Edwin Morgan remarked on the Glasgow photographs in "One Man's World", "Whatever we may learn from statistics or arguments deployed in print about development or redevelopment, it takes the photographer's searching eye, and the silent questions he keeps putting to the bricks and stones, and to people going about their business, to produce images we find ourselves relating to strongly, in terms of thought and feeling. Long may Marzaroli continue to deliver such images." This quotation, with little adaptation, can also apply to William McIlvanney's text.

"Shades of Grey" marks the conjunction of these two substantial talents and their shared experience which is the Glasgow of the past three decades. It is a work which we believe will become a permanent part of Scotland's visual heritage.

Christopher Carrell,
Director, Third Eye Centre

Bill Campbell,
Director, Mainstream Publishing

WHERE GRETA GARBO WOULDN'T HAVE BEEN ALONE

by

WILLIAM McILVANNEY

People trying to be honest will have a clear sense of cities in inverse ratio to time they have spent there. The longer you are acquainted with a place the more you know you don't know it. About New Orleans I'll give you some instant impressions, gleaned in about a week. If you're in a hurry — and if I'm talking about New Orleans, you probably should be — you might be fooled. But five minutes' casual probing would find me out. My clarity about New Orleans is born of ignorance.

Paris I'm more vague about. I wasn't always like that. From a fortnight's trip made as a teenager, I carried a neat sense of it around with me like a postcard. Then I lived there for several months. Don't ask me about Paris. Vancouver's worse. I lived there nearly a year. Glasgow? What I don't know about Glasgow would fill several books. Some people might say it has. What I think and feel about Glasgow, after more than thirty years' close acquaintance, is very involved: the onion, memory. I peel it.

*

The cafeteria of the Students' Union in Glasgow University: evocative place, my Grand Central Station of the mind. From here you can catch ideas that will take you just about anywhere. The condition of the serfs in 19th-century Russia. The pibroch as the essential Scottish art form. Is abortion murder? Arnold Toynbee's *History of the World*. What do you think will win the two-thirty? Was Marlowe Shakespeare? Outline briefly the attributes of your ideal woman. Who was Jack the Ripper?

Here, more than at lectures or tutorials, my mind will be stripped of the fustian of prejudice, the shoddy of preconception, and sent out to abide the pelting of a pitiless storm of wild ideas. It is my subversive university within the University. Maybe I'm particularly lucky in my timing. I arrive here in the mid-fifties, by which time the fabled fortresses of deep thought have been breached by fairly large numbers of working-class students. The Visigoths are here. They bring a refreshing common sense and scepticism to some of the more arcane studies. Anglo Saxon sound changes will take a terrible pounding.

After lectures we convene in the cafe of the Students' Union, often for hours. We have epic conversations. No sacrosanct precept is safe from our desire to scramble all over it and hopefully reduce it to rubble. The size of the group is constantly changing. We can be anything from four round a table to maybe a dozen, with chairs being pulled up and later left empty. New voices arrive from the Reading Room. Someone who has raised an interesting question may have to catch a train before the poll of answers is finally taken. The ashtrays look like pit-bings.

I am among such a group now. I am taking part in an impromptu group lecture on Yeats, whom we read last week. I, who arrived like an urban Johnny Appleseed in the groves of academe, am already towards the end of my first year a sophisticated smoker of Player's (bought in packets of five from the kiosk in the Union), a placer of daily bets with Strachan the bookie (maximum stake: one shilling) and a fearless purveyor of opinion on all matters (knowledge of subject under discussion not an essential).

Around me are my friends. One of them has been reading Freud and is going through a phase of seeing sexuality in all things. A cigarette is a mammary substitute. If you stir your tea, he's liable to accuse you of intercourse in public. Another is developing a betting system that will make his fortune when he becomes a professional gambler. Another is seriously questioning his Catholicism. Another is a Rangers supporter who likes to say that he hates bigotry and Catholics.

But at the moment, everything is concentrated on Yeats. He is our man. We marvel at his wisdom, savour individual lines as if they were nectar. We are endlessly trying to analyse the magic of his words.

At the edge of our group is a rare attender. He comes to university on a motorbike. He is wearing a crash helmet now, perhaps as a protection against the sleet of insubstantial opinion that is all around him. He observes us from his casing like an extra-terrestrial trying to work out what these earthlings are up to. During a rare pause in the conversation, he speaks.

"It's all right for youse bastards," he says. "Youse like poetry."

The inference is that we are cheating. For he, too, is a member of the first year English class and he seems to have a sense of being disadvantaged because some people taking the course are actually enjoying it. This may explain the abstracted way in which he has occasionally sat in on our debates, like a Rabbi attending a course on bacon-curing. It may also explain the infrequency of his visits to lectures. He has opened a second-hand shop, it seems, and he is more interested in driving his motorbike to salerooms all over Glasgow, buying used furniture.

At the end of the academic year, he is refused a class ticket, not surprisingly since the English Department have no very clear idea of who he is. We hold a hurried council of war in the Union and he decides he will go to the English Department and speak to Professor Alexander, a man of great benignity and kindness. When Professor Alexander confronts the non-poetry-loving entrepreneur, accoutred as is customary in his crash-helmet, he apparently says something like this: "With your attendance and performance, sonny, when you come here to ask for a class ticket, you shouldn't be wearing a crash-helmet. You should be wearing a suit of armour."

Professor Alexander, ever humane, gives him a class ticket. But he either doesn't pass the exam or doesn't turn up to sit it — I forget which.

*

Glasgow University was for me not a bad vantage point from which seriously to begin my studies of the city. Unlike some seats of learning, it was no hermetically sealed chamber of self-defining scholarship. It abutted on the very real world. You could step out with a headful of Chaucer and see the Wife of Bath Street on a tram.

I learned more than degree courses during that time. I laid the foundations for a kind of inter-disciplinary study of the place. Glasgow has always been in my experience a city where boundaries are not very rigorously observed, full of socially mixed blood. The forensically precise mind of the lawyer may also accommodate a fanatically irrational belief in the divine right of Celtic to win the Scottish League. A philosophical debate may be resolved with a fist fight.

The crash-helmeted tearaway who was reading selected parts of Spenser's *Faerie Queene* was found to have many counterparts, like the working man playing pool in a Rutherglen pub and simultaneously extolling the quality of *Anna Karenina*. I once had some difficulty escaping from a cab in which the driver hadn't finished outlining his plans for writing a modernised version of *The Ragged Trousered Philanthropists*. At least he turned the meter off. I have heard two drunk men discussing their lives in The Royal Scot bar in Central Station, with one of them insistently quoting Socrates.

Those seminars that began in the Union have continued casually for over thirty years. A group of us have been meeting intermittently in Glasgow pubs, conversationally unravelling our entrails, while jobs were changed and children grew up and marriages broke. We have discussed everything we could think of and a few we probably seriously couldn't. But the sub-text to those discussions has always been Glasgow, and therefore Scotland — for Glasgow, lochs and bens and talk of Gaelic bards notwithstanding, has forged much of the essence of modern Scotland. It reveals most dramatically the basic features not of who we were but of who we are.

Our meetings were often gently haunted by a need to work out Glasgow: to come to terms with the ferocity of its sectarianism, that weird, warped creature that haunts the Scottish psyche, sustaining itself on the iron rations of Rangers-Celtic games and offering meaningless aggression like a Japanese soldier lost for years on some Pacific island and still fighting a war that is long since over; to understand the strong, instinctive socialism of the city, a socialism that seems not to have achieved much that is more concrete than calling a part of itself Nelson Mandela Place and putting up a statue of La Passionaria on Custom House Quay.

But even as we tried to catch the place, it was changing in our grasp, like Proteus.

*

I'm on a late-night train leaving Central Station. I have the compartment to myself until the train begins to pull out. I can hear the scuffling sounds in the corridor outside that announce the man with drink taken who has just made it. Experience tells me he will soon be my travelling companion. He soon is.

He has slid the door open with a force that leaves it jammed. He nods ambiguously, a kind of friendly belligerence. His face is florid, perhaps with running. His eyes are aggressively blank and have a tendency to fix themselves fiercely on a perfectly ordinary object, like an upholstered arm-rest, as if it is the only one of its kind in the world and he will have to report back to a committee on his findings. For a short time our reflections manage to avoid each other in the windows as first the edges of the city, and then the darkened countryside slide past. But I know, short of taking a header through the window, I won't avoid a conversation.

"Just made it there," he says.

I acknowledge the information it seems to have taken him some time to glean and a conversation has begun. It proves to be an interesting conversation. He lives and works in Coventry but comes originally from Glasgow. He has been paying a visit to the old town. His stay there seems to have followed a not uncommon pattern for such visits: quiet at first (seeing his mother, failing to make contact with friends) but building towards a series of jolly thrashes that have climaxed in this evening's impromptu party. Thinking of the party and the time he's just had, he brims with nostalgia.

And then, finding his moment as we rattle through the night in the tatty compartment, he delivers an ambiguous but moving elegy to the Gallowgate. The ambiguity is unintentional. He speaks of the old Gallowgate with a genuine love that few outsiders who have seen it might expect. He sees no irony. He lays the memory of it before me as reverently as a pressed rose. It's just that he doesn't seem to notice that it still has the thorns attached.

The old Gallowgate, he says, was a marvellous place. Everybody helped everybody else. The sense of neighbourliness was total. He is searching for the clincher, the moment held in a shaft of remembered light that will convince even me, find another convert. He decides he has it. It is a story.

This is the story: when he was a boy, he loved snooker. But snooker, say ninepence for half-an-hour, or it may have been one-and-three (he remembered but I don't), was expensive. He and a couple of his mates did devious things and saved up until they had enough money to pay for a half-hour on a table. They were maybe twelve at the time. They duly were given a table. They set up the balls. They chalked the cues. They were ready to break when three local eighteen-year-old heavies cut in. They shoved them away from the table and told them to get lost. They would be playing. He and his mates had no way to deal with the situation. They went outside. A small man that they knew, a local, a "nice wee man", was standing at the door, smoking. He knew they were supposed to be playing a game. They weren't. He asked them why. They told him. The small man went in. Shortly afterwards, they played their full half-hour.

The man on the train speaks of three people "carried out". I doubt that. But I believe the gist of his story.

"That was the Gallowgate," he says in the voice of one who once knew Eden. "Kind people in the Gallowgate."

※

Kind people who batter unkindness — the rose with the thorns. The man from the Gallowgate introduced into our compartment, like a tangible presence, one of the great Glaswegian legends — the hardman — and reminded me how in recent times the sharp edges of the legend have become blurred. The fact that something has become legendary, of course, doesn't mean that it isn't rooted in reality.

Glasgow is a hard town. I know Glaswegians who get instantly annoyed if you say that, their faces acquiring a "here we go again" expression, just as I know New Yorkers who are tired of hearing how dangerous their city is. "Look. I've lived here all my life," a free translation of their general reactions might run. "And I'm lucky if I've seen two fights in that time. Sure there's violence here. But there's violence everywhere."

They have a point. Violence is more dramatic than passivity and, therefore, constitutes a kind of news. Few interesting anecdotes begin, "I was at a Rangers-Celtic game on Saturday and nothing happened. Let me tell you about it". Nevertheless, only people who have observed Glasgow exclusively through the windscreen of a car or who arrange their social diary as a means of censoring their own awareness or who take the pronouncements of the Scottish Tourist Board as hard reportage could pretend that part of the reality of Glasgow has not been a potential for casual violence. The legend may have been fed on the steroids of publicity but it originally earned its muscles on the streets.

There are reasons for it. Glasgow, more dramatically than any other part of Scotland, experienced the brutalising effects of the Industrial Revolution. Edinburgh might partially side-step it by becoming a place where money, more than machinery, was deployed and a centre for tourism. Glasgow stood four-square to the whirlwind. The ensuing varieties of deprivation had their results.

One was the development of a fierce physical pride, fed partly on circumstances that often left room for little else and partly on the democratic traditions deeply embedded in Scottish life. The combination meant that in Glasgow people who frequently didn't have much more collateral than their sense of themselves weren't prepared to have that sense casually burgled by passing strangers. Standing up for yourself, sometimes against improbable odds, became a Glaswegian convention.

The late John Rafferty, sports reporter with the *Scotsman*, used to tell a story of the time when Jacky Paterson, flyweight champion of the world and regarded by many as pound-for-pound the hardest puncher in boxing at the time, was training for a fight. I repeat the story from memory and, if I get it wrong, I apologise to a very fine reporter. The way I recall it, Paterson was training in Glasgow and having trouble making the weight. He was heavily clothed in the gym, trying to sweat off the excess poundage. This meant there was a risk of dehydration and they were having fruit delivered from the Fruit Market. The small man who delivered it looked as if he could make the eight stone flyweight limit with his clothes on. He was pleased to be in the presence of the world champion and became unnecessarily fussy about where he should put the fruit, prolonging his stay and checking with Paterson where exactly he would like the fruit to be. Shipping sweat and understandably irritated, Paterson told him roughly to put the stuff down and get out. The attitude of the fruit-deliverer changed immediately. He was for the jacket off and inviting Paterson to step outside. Nobody spoke to him like that. Only the intervention of John Rafferty and a conciliatory handshake from the world champion mollified the small man.

It hasn't been an entirely malignant convention, though often so. For a long time at least, one aspect of it was a discouragement of casual bullies. When you don't know where the aggression may come from, the quiet man at the bar or the innocent-looking punter in the bus queue, you should walk warily, especially since a lot of Glaswegians are not averse to taking up arms in causes other than their own if they see what they think is an injustice. Even allowing for the fact that memory is a seductive talker who sometimes makes us forget to check his sources, I find the reminiscences of the man from the Gallowgate largely confirmed by personal experience and things I've heard.

While I was teaching, a mature student who had joined the English Department of the school told me about a night in an East End pub. It illustrates what I mean.

There were four students, not from Glasgow. The main protagonist of the story came from Troon, one of those douce — at least on the surface — coastal towns about which I sometimes wonder if they toilet-train the seagulls. Every Thursday the students, in search of the real Glasgow, would have a night in an East End bar. They must have fitted in perfectly, carrying their briefcases.

This night they were drinking at the counter and listening to Engelbert Humperdinck on the television singing *The Last Waltz*. The man from Troon started to sing along and, noticing a woman sitting in a corner singing too, he began to harmonise with her. The woman was amused. Her large male companion was not. He came across and demanded that the student come outside with him, presumably regarding singing with his woman as some kind of sexual approach. The student at first, not unwisely, refused. But he found himself outside anyway with the large man saying very severe things about what was going to happen to him.

But another man had followed them out from the bar. He forbade the large man to touch the student and produced from his coat pocket, as a reinforcement of his point of view, a hammer. The large man withdrew. The man with the hammer was reported to me as saying then, "Now, son. You go back in there an' have a right good night." The student apparently remembered he had a train to catch.

Robin Hoods with hammers in their hands are probably less likely in Glasgow these days. It's always hard to gauge the changing temper of the times in these matters but the very fallible readings that emerge from newspapers and talk and personal experience would appear to suggest that there has been an erosion of the admittedly confused ethic of the non-criminal hardman. Drugs may well have played a part in that.

But perhaps just as significant a reason for the apparent decay of honour among hardmen is the sub-theme in the talk of the man from the Gallowgate: the dispersal of the sense of community. The post-war annihilation of the tenement in Glasgow wiped out not only buildings but a way of life. As Bertie Auld, then manager of Partick Thistle, once said, "If they'd given Hitler the contract, he couldn't have done a better job." Often what was put in their place suggested a novel interpretation of "progress".

Outside Queen Elizabeth Court on the South Side: there's a photographer and a young journalist and myself. We're looking for high views of the city to go with a piece in the *Glasgow Herald*. The concrete block of flats looks good as a place from which to take photographs. But that's all it looks good for. I can't believe that this building has been conceived as an improvement. An improvement on what? Alcatraz? The journalist is telling me that this sort of work has won an architectural award for Sir Basil Spence. He does not specify which award. It was presumably the Bomber Harris award for architecture, since it looks like vertical rubble.

We go inside. Outside the lift, two older women, a younger woman and two boys are waiting. The boys are playing keepie-uppie headers with a tennis ball. They don't look ready for the first team. The ball has a dangerous tendency to wander close to other people. One of the older women promises mayhem if the ball so much as touches her.

"No problem, missus," one of the boys says unconvincingly.

On the way up in the lift, they all leave except the young woman and the three of us. We talk to her, explaining what we're here for. We want to get out on to the roof. She's visiting her mother on the top floor and knows that there's a door out to the roof but she doesn't think it will be open. It's kept locked for obvious reasons. On the top floor she directs us to where the door is and goes into her mother's.

We find the door and the young woman is right: it's locked. As we're wandering back along the corridor, thinking janitors and jemmies, the young woman is standing outside an open door. She is signalling the three of us in. She has mentioned us to her mother and they both wonder if we couldn't use their balcony to get our photographs. We could.

Ensues a happy time. We take our photogrpahs. We come back in to cups of tea and biscuits. We talk for almost an hour of governments and high-rise flats and how the family's doing. We look at the album of the daughter's trip to Canada to see her sister and her family. We're all pleased that they're doing so well out there.

These are impressive people. They're trusting. They make us feel instantly that we have a right to be here. As we leave, the mother says to be sure and look in again if we're passing. The whole occasion is an unexpected gift from strangers. Never mind the photos, I'm just glad I came.

✳

The woman and her daughter were practising an old Glaswegian art form: the transformation of your circumstances with humour and pride. Never mind the building, see the people. It's a skill in which the people of Glasgow have had to become expert. It's also a skill which has been under increasing pressure over the past forty years.

A lot of the old tenements were hardly fit to live in but they did have a strong sense of community. Changes had to be made but they were frequently made by people who seemed to have all the imagination of a soldier ant. Mainly, what had been fairly coherent communities were either shipped out to housing schemes like penal colonies on the edges of the city or incarcerated in high-rise flats. Presumably, they had committed being working class. The buildings themselves usually looked like the result of some Dada school of architecture, cunningly created with built-in obsolescence, so that they would turn scabrous in ten years or so.

The philosophy, shared supposedly by a lot of Labour councillors who should have known better, appeared to be that working-class aspirations stopped at the inside toilet. The malignant implication behind it was that there was no such thing as a working-class culture and, therefore, nothing would be lost by thoughtlessly unstitching the fabric of a way of life put together over generations.

However unintentionally, that attitude suggests contempt and contempt makes distance between people. The distances that housing policy helped to create were not just geographical.

*

La Lanterna, Italian restaurant in Hope Street: three of us at table. The waiter brings the menu. One of us is distinctly fidgety. He studies the red-checked tablecloth, the cutlery, the surroundings. He shifts his position in his seat. He lifts the menu and glances at it, puts it back down. He shakes his head. His unease is uncontainable.

"Ah'll have tae go, Wullie," he says.

"What's the problem?"

"Nah, this is no' for me. No way. Ah canny sit here."

We all rise and make our apologies and go out. We look for a less intimidating place to eat. The fidgety man is Hughie, a friend of mine from Possilpark, and I have just demonstrated how socially insensitive I can be.

I have recently been spending some time in Possil, trying to understand what's happening there, however inadequately. What's happening there wouldn't be out of place in *Last Exit to Brooklyn*. I've found how freely heroin is available in pubs, how protection is rife, how just about any article within reason can be ordered at lunchtime and delivered at tea-time, having been stolen in the afternoon. I've met a girl who was raped at fourteen and soon after turned on to heroin by her addict brothers and put on the streets to feed all their habits. I've met a former social worker so shell-shocked by what he had to deal with that he outlines a scheme whereby local tearaways would be given handouts to buy good suits so that when they go to Bearsden to break into houses they won't be conspicuous. I study his face for irony but am not convinced I see it. I've also met a lot of good local people whose decency seems incredible, given the circumstances they live among. I've stayed overnight at Hughie and Annie's house with another friend, enjoying a few drinks, homemade soup and a sing-song.

The Italian restaurant was my way of offering a gesture of thanks but Annie couldn't make it. I was at first surprised by Hughie's reaction in the restaurant. And then I was surprised at my surprise. I should have known. Eating out is not what Hughie does.

My surprise gave way to annoyance at myself for forgetting for the moment where I come from. If anyone should have foreseen Hughie's attitude, it should have been myself. All I had to do was remember my own former awkwardness in such places, an awkwardness that can ambush me occasionally still and makes me regress to those times when I sat at weddings determined not to be the first at the table to start on the next course.

But it was a salutary experience, a neat hook on which to hang my awareness of that other Glasgow that lies behind the increasingly yuppie image of the city. I had noticed the outriders of that image some time before.

*

A group of us go one night for a drink in The Gay Gordon, a downstairs pub in Royal Exchange Square. We feel slightly out of touch with that part of the city and will renew our acquaintance with old haunts. The bar is closed and the exterior is concealed behind the wrappings that denote renovation. We go off, muttering vaguely among ourselves, and have a drink elsewhere.

Another night we come back and behold the transformation. What was The Gay Gordon, a pleasantly scruffy talking shop, is now a French restaurant called, if I recall, L'Auberge. (It has changed since.) Upstairs is something called Charlie Parker's. We stare at the new black chic door and look at one another, feeling our arteries harden. We push open the door and are confronted by two very tall young men who have the threatening suavity that seems to earn you your bouncer's card these days, as if they have been to karate finishing school. Whatever obscure test it is these gentleman are taught to apply, clean collar, deodorised oxters or a full set of teeth, we seem to pass it. We are allowed to enter the sanctum.

Gloom, not only ours, abounds. Nearly everything, furniture, bar, ceiling, walls, seems to be black. There is even a black bandstand, peopled by black metallic figures. There is one emaciated figure with a saxophone attached. This is presumably "Bird" himself, living up to his nickname — in this case maybe a heron or flamingo. My first impression, admittedly perhaps rancorous with the apprehended encroachment of old age, is that this is somebody's confused impression of a speakeasy remembered from the back row of the pictures during a heavy necking session.

But it is not the place so much that makes us grope abstractedly for our Rip Van Winkle beards and wonder where we have been during the last several years. It is the people. Where do they come from, these people? This is Glasgow?

They are mainly young and dressed in an interesting variety of styles but, no matter how eclectic the gear they wear, what they are all mainly dressed in is a kind of hand-me-down self-assurance. They know they're with it because their clothes are with it. They're sure of their identity because they're wearing it. By pushing open a door, a group of post-war conversational artisans have found that the age of the poser is upon them.

For these people are here to be seen, not to debate the failure of socialism for three hours over a beer-stained table and then apply old songs like bandages to the mental wounds. They stand with their interesting clothes and their different drinks and laugh tunefully and count the house. The phrase that keeps forcing itself into my mind, as I survey the scene like one of Yeats's wrinkled men in *Lapis Lazuli*, is communal pretentiousness. Showing off on such a scale and in such borrowed styles (gallusness is one thing) is not something I have expected to see in Glasgow, which has always seemed to me to be to pretentiousness what Wimpey was to empty houses. We stand around for a while, like people waiting for a bus that doesn't pass this way any longer, and pay what we feel are inflated prices and talk in an awkward, conspiratorial fashion, as if ideas might be contraband. Then we repair to an older bar where people talk to strangers they don't want to pick up.

Being an insistently analytical group, we all have theories. The disco, that peculiarly modern art form where living statuary meets and attracts mainly by gesture and stance, has invaded the pub. Just as the old humanising and individualising patter of the dancing seems to be going largely by the board, so maybe the pub as talking shop is under threat. Innocence has gone. You can't call a pub "Gay" any more. The American influence has always been strong in Glasgow. We have seen the future and it's largely kitsch.

*

We were over-reacting of course. Isn't that what pubs give you a licence to do? The truth was that not only had Glasgow been changing, so had we with it. And I have since developed a certain affection for Charlie Parker's for I once had a life-affecting lunch in there. Any place can be transformed by circumstances.

But that night remains important in my understanding of Glasgow and the door into Charlie Parker's led to a couple of reminders about the place. Firstly, the city always has been changing significantly since I've known it, whether in the big ways like the miles of internal motorway and the Gorbals becoming a different place or in the small ways like Alice's Restaurant disappearing or the amazing acrobatic fiddler in St Enoch's Square giving way to the one-man Wham Bam Boogie Band. You glance away for a month or two from a place you've known and you look back at a stranger. Writing about the city and wanting to use real places in a novel, I have had to keep checking, between conception and execution, that the places were still there.

Secondly, I was reminded of what is the essential direction of that change. It has been a movement, superficially at least, towards a softer image. That's all right, as far as it goes. The question is: how far does it go?

It's good that people should realise how architecturally beautiful Glasgow is. The handsomeness of the city has too often been underplayed. It's good that the fever for demolition seems to have passed its crisis and some of the fine tenements are being refurbished instead of destroyed. It's good that the Merchant City and some points further east begin to flourish again. But there's a danger in handing Glasgow over lock, stock and Burrell to the brochure writers.

Many of those who bemoan the old exaggerated image of Glasgow as a kind of Somme in civvies are busy giving it a press that is just as phoney. That is bad news in two ways.

First, to gloss over the existence of a problem is to feed the problem. Cosmetic surgery never cured a cancer. "Glasgow's Miles Better"? It depends which direction you go in. If you head towards Possil or Blackhill or Easterhouse or Garthamlock or Drumchapel, you couldn't take that ad-man's slogan as more than an ad-man's slogan. And if you're not prepared to go in these directions, you're missing Glasgow.

Second, the selling of Glasgow as some sort of yuppie freehold is a diminution of Glasgow. It's a lot more than that. It's fine that business and tourism should come to the city — as long as the terms are right — but let's not confuse the press release with the reality. The reality is much more complex. Glasgow is a great city. Glasgow is in trouble. Glasgow is handsome. Glasgow is ugly. Glasgow is kind. Glasgow is cruel. Some people in Glasgow live full and enlightened lives. Some people in Glasgow live lives bleaker than anyone should live — and die deaths bleaker than anyone should die.

*

I am sitting in my reasonably grotty Glasgow bedsit being a writer. I have done my statutory spell of staring at the wall. I am now making notes towards making notes that may lead to an idea that may lead, eventually, to the clarification of what it is I want to say. Then perhaps work can begin.

Outside it is a dull day. But, given the state of my windows, any day looked at from here is going to be a dull day. To be absolutely accurate about the quality of the weather, I'd have to go out and check.

There is a knock at the door. This is unusual. Apart from the fact that my self-imposed isolation has been making me feel recently like a one-man leper colony, my bedsit is in one of those divided Victorian houses. What was presumably one big happy family has become a series of separate units where some students and other migrants and myself hang out. I know them mainly as people nodding on the stairs and records playing and flushing cisterns and ghostly ripples of half-heard laughter. But the point is that our divided household means a list of names outside and a series of bell-pushes and one of those crackly devices through which you identify yourself as not being a mugger.

So who can it be? It must be somebody from inside the building. I suppose the best way to find out is to open the door.

It is a woman I have never seen before. She has a small girl hovering at her side.

"Could ye dae me a favour, son?" she says.

Any half-baked quips about women always appearing at my door with such requests are forestalled by my sense that something is wrong. Later, I'll be glad they were. The small girl is the sign. She is ill at ease without seeming to know why, in that instinctive geiger-counter way that children have.

"Certainly, love. What is it?"

The woman is already moving away, talking as she does so, with the small girl holding her hand. When I'm asked to surface quickly out of work, it can take me a while to focus. I'm not entirely sure where I am, I tend only to hear part of what's being said. I won't say I'm coming back from a deep place but certainly a far one. I'm like that now. The woman is leading me through the open door of a flat and talking. It will only be in retrospect that I'll be able to decide clearly what she has been telling me.

It's about wee Tommy being the tenant of the flat and she cleans it for him and he's out at work just now but last night he had somebody staying with him who was drunk and he was still there this morning and Tommy phoned her and told her to make sure the man was out by the time she left but the man still seems to be drunk and could I help her to get him out?

It sounds like a commission not without its risks.

"He's in there," she says, pointing to a bedroom door that is ajar.

There's the woman and the small girl and myself. It's John Wayne time. I go into the bedroom. At first I don't see him. The bed is mussed but empty. Then I see him. He's in underpants and tee-shirt. He's lying on the floor, quite still. He is a short and powerful man, say late twenties, with dark curly hair. There's a record player on the floor beside him and his right hand is poised over it in a strange way. His head is slightly under a sideboard. It looks as if he's passed out while putting on a record. I cross towards him and bend and touch his shoulder. It feels like cement.

"Excuse me," I'm saying ridiculously.

I can hear the girl beginning to cry out in the hallway. The woman is standing at the door. I try to look into his face and I touch his head gently. The hair is very cold.

"He's dead, love," I hear myself saying and the woman begins to cry as well.

I say we have to get the police and does she want me to phone. The woman says no, if somebody has to stay here it won't be her and the girl. She'll phone the police. While she does so, I realise that what I had thought was an identity-bracelet was a piece of wire round his wrist with a ring of blackened skin beneath it. I realise that he wasn't changing a record. He was plugging himself into the socket.

Later, during questioning, a policeman, who knows my occupation says, "You're our first suspect. We think you did it to write about it." Later still, at the inquest in the Sheriff Court, I'm shown photographs of the dead man with his tee-shirt off and can see how he has wrapped himself round and round with wires. I'm asked what kind of shoes I was wearing at the time. They were rubber-soled. It's a good thing for me, it seems. The dead man was, ironically, live and I had two chances at being electrocuted.

In the time between the finding of the body and the inquest, I will think about the dead man quite a lot. But on the evening of the day of touching the utterly innocent coldness of his head, I just go out alone into Glasgow. I get drunk.

*

The calculated savagery of the young man's act against himself was appalling. So, imaginably, was the loneliness that led him to do it: the sewers of self-contempt he must have crawled through to bring himself to the place where he wrapped himself so meticulously in his own death that there would be no possibility of escape; the utter absence he must have felt of anyone with whom he could share the bleakness he had come to.

His action expressed a condition so extreme as to appear eccentric, a grotesquerie of experience faced with which all you could do was turn away. But only the extremity was eccentric. Milder forms of the loneliness that became in him terminal were observable all around. Thinking of him, I thought also of the lesser species of loneliness in the city: not just the more obvious ones like the bearded winos who seem to have taken a short-cut to old age and make you wonder where they come from (being, as my mother would say, "somebody's rearin") or those descendants of the ancient mariner who wander companionless streets imparting urgent gibberish to the world, but also the more discreet and self-contained lonelinesses of people in damp basement flats and hardboard-partitioned bedsits who tend fragile hopes like potted plants.

That, too, is Glasgow. In my quite wilful map of the city, I tend to place them roughly around the Byres Road area, in Hyndland and behind the Botanic Gardens and off Great Western Road. They are dreamers of small, lonely dreams. I remember a conversation in a café in Byres Road with a young man who had read something I had written and who recognised me. He came across and we talked for maybe half-an-hour. He was living in a bedsit with his girlfriend and doing, I think, translations from Spanish and wanting to be a writer. Our talk was for me a peephole into a fierce and private obsession sustained on meals that came pre-cooked in tinfoil and long talks into the night. I remember a late night with a taxi-driver friend and his mates in a room with bean-bag seats and posters on the wall, and a joint circulating, and the names of foreign cities evoking a future that would be different from this. I remember a flat in Hyndland where I turned up with an ex-fisherman I know and all the Highland voices were melodiously evoking images in haunting contrast to the city outside.

The dead man in the bedroom reminded me of such places and such times and later I tried to put the feelings in a poem I called *Bless this house: a sampler for Glasgow bedsits.*

*

Bless this house, wherever it is,
This house and this and this and this

Pitched shaky as small nomad tents
Within Victorian permanence

Where no names stay long, no families meet
In Observatory Road and Clouston Street

Where Harry and Sally who want to be "free"
And Morag who works in the BBC

And Andy the Artist and Mhairi and Fran
(Whose father will never understand)

And John from Kilmarnock and Jean from the Isles
And Michael who jogs ever day for miles

And Elspeth are passing through this year:
Bless them the short time they are here.

Bless the cup left for a month or more
On the dust of the window-ledge, the door

That won't quite shut, the broken fan,
The snowscape of fat in the frying pan.

Bless each burnt chop, each unseen smile
That they may nourish their hopes a while.

Bless the persistence of their faith,
The gentle incense of their breath.

Bless the wild dreams that are seeded here,
The lover to come, the amazing career.

Bless such small truths as they may find
By the lonely night-light of the mind.

Bless these who camp out in the loss of the past
And scavenge their own from what others have lost,

Who have courage to reach for what they cannot see
And have gambled what was for what may never be.

So turn up the Hi Fi, Michael and John.
What is to come may be already gone.

And pull up the covers, Jean and Mhairi.
The island is far and you've missed the ferry.

*

The thoughts provoked by finding the man dead crystallised another small awareness. The man was Iranian. Rumours circulated about why he had taken his life. One theory was that his parents were still in Iran and he was in despair about what would happen to them under the Ayatollah. Whatever lay behind his death, it reminded me of the smaller ethnic groups that enrich the city and tend too often to be overlooked when those who love the place are taking a conversational census of its characteristics.

I thought of the musically named Ladipo Banjo, whom I had known at university. Thinking of him, I found myself guilty of that same oversight. I knew Ladipo was African. I thought he was Nigerian but I wasn't sure. All I could be definite about in my memory was that he was marvellously sweet-natured.

I thought of drinking coffee and discussing being a Pakistani in Scotland with Ahmed Choudry in his leather shop near Partick Cross. I remembered the late Jonathan Meadows, an intense and intelligent man whom I had met in a bar when he couldn't resist joining in a discussion a group of us were having about Norman Mailer. We became friends and he gave me some insights into the experience of the Jewish community in Glasgow. I thought of the Poles and the Italians and the Chinese. I thought of the Irish, whose positive contribution to the nature of Glasgow and of Scottishness is so deeply ingrained that its importance is often overlooked.

It's no wonder Glasgow is such a vivid city, ready to surprise you at any time.

*

It is raining at the taxi-rank opposite the Botanic Gardens. It is doubtless raining in many other places as well but this is the only one I'm interested in at the moment. I don't have a coat on and turning up my jacket collar is no substitute. I'm cold and wet and getting wetter. Everything seems dark, including my mood.

A taxi comes off Great Western Road and makes a u-turn into the rank. I climb in, discontinuing my mental tirade against all Glasgow taxi-drivers and reflecting more charitably on the number of times in my experience hackney cabs have justified their Glaswegian nickname of "black ambulances". I tell the driver my destination and we set off through grey rain, along grey streets, under a grey sky. The driver studies me in the rearview mirror with the eyes of man who has never lost his curiosity about things.

"Have ye ever wondered," he says, his eyes still flicking on to me more frequently than seems consistent with maximum concentration on his driving. "Have ye ever wondered whit would win in a fight between a crocodile and a shark?"

I am, as they say, nonplussed. In all my deep ponderings on the world and its many manifestations, this is one I've missed. It seems such a natural, even inevitable question the way the taxi-driver says it, I can't imagine why I've never asked it myself. Shamefacedly, I acknowledge how unthinking my progress through life has so far been.

"It's an amazin' thing," he says. "Ah'm sittin' in the hoose the other night readin' a book. An' Ah shouts to the wife, 'Hey, hen. See the way Ah'm always sayin', "Ah wonder what would win between a crocodile an' a shark?" (I have an eerie flash of the kind of conversations that must take place in his house: "See's ower the paper, hen. Bet ye there's nothin' in it aboot crocodiles an' sharks the day again.") 'Well, here's the answer here.'"

I sit tensed in the back of the cab, no longer a mere traveller to an address but a journeyor into esoteric knowledge. But the taxi-driver, like all true gurus, knows that the path to wisdom is a winding one.

"Seems there's this river in Australia. Right? An' at the mouth of it ye've got yer crocodiles. An' then yer sharks are swimmin' in. Into the estuary, like. Fair enough. Wallop. A square go."

He seems to need for the first time to concentrate totally on a tricky piece of steering. He knows he has me. I try to ask him nonchalantly, to make sure my voice isn't quavering with suppressed emotion.

"So what would win?"

He glances at me in the mirror, looks at the road.

"Ah suppose it's obvious when ye think about it," he says. "The crocodile. Seems it bides its time, one bite, hold on, ta ta shark."

So there we are, another nibble at the infinite apple of knowledge. Brooding in my back seat, I decide daringly — for David Attenborough I'm not and what do I know about crocodiles and sharks? — that I don't believe him. Isn't it true, my scepticism is whispering like a wee boy in the back row of the class, that crocodiles are freshwater creatures?

But I am very glad he told me. He has, as the poet says, saved some part of a day I had rued. We've been exploring to other climes, he and I, however briefly. The rain receded just then and it was like the moment when Dorothy leaves the black and white farm and walks into the technicolour of her search for Oz.

*

The memory of such experiences brings me nearer to the essence of my sense of Glasgow. No matter what harsh anomalies I find in the city, no matter what misgivings I may have about what's happening to it, no matter what changes overtake and alter what I thought was final, a moment like that is a familiar landmark and I recognise the place again.

I stood once at the bar of the Gowdoc in Great Western Road, feeling like a tortoise that had just been de-shelled. I no longer remember what troubles I had then but I had decided they were big ones. I was standing in for Atlas. Nobody knows the trouble I've seen. A small man at the bar beside me suddenly spoke.

"How's it gaun, big yin? Ye don't look that happy. You think you've got problems? Listen."

It seemed that a few days ago he had met a friend he hadn't seen for years. They had gone on the skite together and the wee man hadn't been home for nights, three, I think it was. He was asking my advice. Should he go home tonight or, since he was bound to get laldy anyway, should he have another night at it?

Always at such times I know that this is Glasgow: land of the unsolicited confidentiality, country of the unasked for information, city where Greta Garbo wouldn't have been allowed to be alone — "Who's the big wumman wi' the funny hat? Get ower here, ya big stoater, an' jine the comp'ny. Charlie, gie 'er a pina colada."

※

It is lunchtime in The Horsehose Bar in Drury Street. Several tall lights on tripods have been focused on one of the wooden tables. A man sits at the table with his back to the door. A television camera has been set up. It is trained on the door into the bar.

My moment has come. For I will be entering through that door. The camera will catch me as I enter, follow me to the bar, where I will order a drink, and doggedly pursue me as I sit down at the table opposite the man with his back to the camera. The interview will begin. It is for a film about Glasgow to be shown in West Germany.

I stand outside, waiting for the shouted signal. It's just like being in the pictures, isn't it? This is really a kind of acting, isn't it? I hope the rain doesn't plaster my hair to my head the way it usually does, making it look like a greasy balaclava. "Okay!" Camera, action, shoot.

I enter. I walk over to the bar in a manner I hope is casual and ask for a whisky. The manager, who has obviously given us permission to invade his bar in the first place, smiles and hands me a huge whisky which he has had sitting ready under the counter. My quest for method-school naturalness, an inhabiting of the part, is thrown by this. Why not use the optic? I have reached into my pocket and pulled out some money but the manager smiles again and turns away, commendably refusing to hog the camera. But what do I do with the money? Donate it to charity? I put it back in my pocket.

By this time, as I stumble towards the table, I feel the omens are not propitious for an interview in which I'm supposed to try to give a real sense of Glasgow. We've already, in about twenty seconds, managed to depict Glasgow as a city where casual strangers entering a bar are given bowls of free whisky. I envisage legions of outraged German tourists picketing Glaswegian pubs. I sit down and nod to my interviewer, who smiles reassuringly back. Even this part, now that I'm doing it, feels daft to me. Won't it convey the impression that people meeting for the first time in Glasgow bars conduct interviews with each other? But it's not my programme.

"Tell me," my interviewer says, "what, do you think, is the special quality Glasgow bars like this have? What's typical of them?"

This is probably my chance to explain that what has just happened isn't typical and that, for example, you usually have to pay for the drink. But the remorseless eye of the camera is on us and I chicken out. Instead, I go into a spiel about the communal nature of at least some Glasgow pubs, the likelihood of being engaged in conversation, of having your privacy benignly invaded, of being interrupted — at which exact point I'm aware of a shadow across our table and the lighting man dancing like a dervish in the background and I hear a voice saying: "Oh-ho, whit's gaun on here, then?"

A fairly elderly man has joined us at the table and is interviewing the interviewer. The interviewer is English and there seems to be some language difficulty. Offering my services, I ask the man what the problem is.

"Oh, no problem, son," he says, his eyes assessing what size of coffin I'll require. "Ah jist want tae know whit's gaun on here."

We continue talking and, while he studies the lights and checks out the television crew, I explain that we're conducting an interview.

"Interview?" He holds up a stiff, leather-gloved hand that is obviously made of something other than flesh. "Interview? Ah'll gie ye an interview. How about interviewin' the war-wounded?"

*

The man said more, much more. I've never seen the finished film but I understand the director intended to cut that moment of interruption. Certainly, the cameraman stopped filming very quickly, which was a pity. The scene was Glasgow in action, far more eloquent than any conversation we could have had.

The man wasn't just the incarnation of the point I had been trying to make. He was an interesting user of Glasgow speech, that aspect of the city in which I see most hope for the survival of its identity undiluted.

For Glasgow's soul is in its mouth. Anyone who wants a quick and painless introduction to the essential Glasgow should read Michael Munro's excellent dictionary of Glasgow speech, *The Patter*, full of superbly creative examples.

Even a cursory acquaintance with that speech will reveal that it is not merely a collection of slightly different words. It is the expression of a coherent attitude to life, a series of verbal stances as ritualised as one of the martial arts. But it is also continuingly inventive, an established style within which individual creativity can flourish.

The salient features of that style emerged directly from the hardness of life in the streets of a major industrial city. Such a life demands the frequent application of painkillers and so there are many ways in which you can be drunk. You can be wellied, plootered, steamboats or blootered, among others. Drunkenness can lead to insults and the designation of someone as a bawheid, a doughheid, a chanty-wrastler, a heid-banger or a bampot whose patter's mince. Insults beget violence and you may find yourself banjoed or burst or rattled or melted or invited to come ahead.

But, in fact, many Glaswegian insults and threats are as much a way of containing violence as of causing it. They are like the warning signals animals emit. Perhaps part of the reason for Glasgow's reputation for being a threatening city is that much of the violence has been codified into speech that is highly skilled in drawing demarcation lines of behaviour. These can make certain conversations a complex map of grid-lines and markings the wise cartographer can interpret: "No Go Area", "Dead End", "Bears Crossing".

But these are the outer edges of the significance of Glaswegian speech. The core of its style is two main qualities: deflation of pomposity and humour. It's hard to be pompous when you have a geggie for a mouth and a bahookie for a posterior. The humour takes many forms but I believe that the commonest of these is the humour of disgruntlement — that central source of laughter to which we have been led by such diverse practitioners as Evelyn Waugh, Groucho Marx and Woody Allen. So much of Glasgow humour is disbelief under anaesthetic. It is anger with the fuse snuffed but still smoking.

Glasgow speech, like so much of Glasgow itself, expresses partly incredulity at what life offers, partly a way to make the best of things, partly an invitation to seize the moment and to hell with the formalities.

*

The late-night train has left Waverley Station in Edinburgh and is headed towards Glasgow Queen Street. I am slouched in my seat, flagellating myself silently for another failed Festival. Every year I go through determined this time to gorge myself on the arts. Every year I retreat feeling culturally emaciated. It's the sheer number of possibilities on offer that always paralyses me: so many exhibitions, recitals, plays, films, so many Fringe shows in out-of-the-way places that are "stunning" and "magical" and "riotously funny". I usually end up as one of an audience of nine, trying to remember where I read the review that was presumably written by the actors and wondering where the action is. It's always fun to go there but is it art? This year has been no exception.

The door to the compartment opens and two women in their forties enter. One of them is calling to someone behind her: "Come oan in here, hen. They're a' snobs through there." They are followed by a girl carrying a violin-case., Throughout the long car, somnolent people quicken into apprehension, knowing that, whatever is going to happen, this is not part of the normal service of British Rail.

"Right, hen," one of the women says. "You sit here an' gie's a wee tune."

The girl unlocks the lid of the case and, removing a violin from its velvet bedding, transforms it instantly to a fiddle in her hands. A spontaneous ceilidh occurs. Music, that old subversive of the senses, insinuates its way past inhibitions and darts like a pyromaniac from person to person, igniting faces into smiles. Hands clap. Heads bob rhythmically. The place is jumping. There is dancing in the aisle. Whirling there with a black man she has unceremoniously "lifted", one of the women shouts to me: "Ever had two Blue Lagoons? This is what they do for ye."

The jollity continues until we have almost reached Glasgow. Then the two women go round the compartment taking a collection for the girl. She makes a nice bit of money. As we pull into Queen Street, I realise that Glasgow has had its own unofficial mini-festival.

❋

If someone has a violin, you say to them, "Gie's a tune". If a dignified black man is sitting on a train, you get him up to dance. If you've had a drink, you announce it to anyone who'll listen. If you think a young girl deserves some money, you take a collection from a carriageful of strangers.

The core of the onion. Does an onion have a core? This one does. I come at last to the heart of my Glasgow, boil it down and freeze it in two words: humane irreverence. Those who are, for me, the truest Glaswegians, the inheritors of the tradition, the keepers of the faith, are terrible insisters that you don't lose touch for a second with your common humanity, that you don't get above yourself. They refuse to be intimidated by professional status or reputation or attitude or name. But they can put you down with a style that almost constitutes a kindness.

A group of us are leaving Hampden after an international match. There's my son, three policemen, Sean Connery and myself. I've met Connery only twice before, once when I interviewed him in the Dorchester Hotel and once, in a James Bond way, at Edinburgh Zoo, where he talked of trying to get the money together to film one of my books, *Laidlaw*. But with the authentic charm that he has, he has connected as if we all saw one another last week. We're going to run him to the airport to catch an early flight. We're talking and trying to find the car, which has been parked some way from the ground.

"I can't believe I'm here," Connery says. "I'm sitting in 'Tramps' at two o'clock this morning when Rod Stewart walks in. He's chartered a private plane and why don't I come to the game. So here I am."

It's a straight enough statement, just a genuine expression of surprise at the way things have happened. Sean Connery doesn't need to drop names. But, anyway, one of the policemen puts one quietly in the post for him.

"Aye," he says. "It's a small world, big yin. Ah was in a house at Muirheid at two o'clock this mornin'. It was full o' tramps as well."

The man who says this comes, in fact, from Ayrshire but he has been a policeman in Glasgow for years, is an honorary Glaswegian. And he picked the right place to say it.

Humane irreverence: more than the big ships, Glasgow's greatest export. I just hope they don't export it all away. May the Mitchell Library, now so handsomely refurbished, always have its quota of sceptical readers finding out for themselves, noseying into things that are supposed to be none of their business. May the Citizens' Theatre and the Tron and the King's and, yea, even Scottish Opera always find among their audiences some of those perennially disgruntled faces that could be captioned: "They ca' this art?". May the Burrell and the Glasgow Art Gallery and the Third Eye Centre always have their equivalent of the wee man I once saw standing before "Le Christ", seeming to defy Salvador Dali to justify himself and shaking his head and glancing round, as if looking for support. For if they go, Glasgow, except for the bricks, goes with them.

They — not the image-makers, not the bright-eyed entrepreneurs, not those who know the city as a taxi-ride between a theatre and a wine-bar, not those who see it as Edinburgh on the Clyde, not the literary cliques, not those who apply the word "renaissance" to a handful of movies and a few books of poetry and some novels and plays — they are the heart of Glasgow: the quizzical starers, the cocky walkers, the chic girls who don't see a phoney accent as an essential accessory of attractiveness, the askers of questions where none was expected, the dancers on the train, the strikers-up of unsolicited conversations, the welcomers of strangers, the deliverers of deadly lines in most unlikely places, the people fighting decency's rearguard action in Possil, the unpretentious, the unintimidated. Glasgow belongs to them.

Photographs by

OSCAR MARZAROLI

CITYSCAPES
Previous page
JOHN KNOX OVERLOOKING THE NECROPOLIS, 1964
Upper
NECROPOLIS SKYLINE, 1966
Lower
ROYAL INFIRMARY SKYLINE, 1966
Opposite
GLASGOW CATHEDRAL, 1986

CITYSCAPES
Upper
LOOKING SOUTH FROM PARK TERRACE, 1960
Lower
BRIDGES ON THE RIVER CLYDE, 1963

CITYSCAPES
Upper
WINTER ON THE RIVER CLYDE, 1982
Lower
SUSPENSION BRIDGE, RIVER CLYDE, 1981

43

CITYSCAPES
Upper
LOOKING SOUTH FROM THE ROYSTON FLATS, 1963
Lower
SPRINGBURN, 1963

CITYSCAPES
Upper
RIVER KELVIN NEAR KELVIN HALL, 1965
Middle
WOMAN ON BRIDGE, FORTH AND CLYDE CANAL, 1965
Lower
PHOENIX PARK, 1965

45

CITYSCAPES
ST ROLLOX FROM ROYSTON FLATS, 1963

46

CITYSCAPES
Upper left
GEORGE SQUARE, 1966
Upper right
GLASGOW UNIVERSITY AND STATUE OF FIELD MARSHAL EARL ROBERTS, 1976
Lower
GLASGOW ART GALLERY AND MUSEUM, 1970

47

CITYSCAPES
Upper
GLASGOW SCHOOL OF ART FROM THE REAR, 1968
Lower
GLASGOW SCHOOL OF ART, 1968

CITYSCAPES
Upper
PAVILION THEATRE, RENFIELD STREET, 1982
Middle
LUNCHEON AND TEA ROOMS, GREAT WESTERN ROAD, 1982
Lower
COLOSSEUM BUILDING, JAMAICA STREET, 1985

49

CITYSCAPES
Upper left
NEWTON TERRACE, 1986
Upper right
CLAREMONT TERRACE, 1986
Lower
TRINITY COLLEGE TOWERS, 1986

50

THE CLYDE/SHIPBUILDING
Previous page
HOPPER ON THE CLYDE NEAR COLVILLES ORE TERMINAL, 1965
Upper
JOHN BROWNS, 1960
Lower
WELDING, FAIRFIELDS, 1968
Opposite
QUEEN ELIZABETH II PRIOR TO LAUNCH AT JOHN BROWNS, 1967

THE CLYDE/SHIPBUILDING
Upper
CRANES AT JOHN BROWNS, 1966
Lower
QUEEN ELIZABETH II ON THE STOCKS, JOHN BROWNS, 1966

THE CLYDE/SHIPBUILDING
Upper
PREPARING FOR LAUNCH AT FAIRFIELDS, 1965
Lower
LAUNCHING AT FAIRFIELDS, 1965

THE CLYDE/SHIPBUILDING
Upper
CRANES AT HARLAND AND WOLFF, GOVAN, 1964
Lower
SITE OF HARLAND AND WOLFF AFTER CLEARING, GOVAN, 1965

THE CLYDE/SHIPBUILDING
Upper
FERRYMAN, FINNIESTON FERRY, 1977
Lower
FINNIESTON FERRY, 1977

THE CLYDE/SHIPBUILDING
Upper
P.S. WAVERLEY ON THE FROZEN CLYDE, ANDERSTON QUAY, 1982
Lower
FINNIESTON CRANE, THE CLYDE, 1986

STEEL
FURNACE MEN, RAVENSCRAIG STEELWORKS, 1962

STEEL
POURING STEEL, RAVENSCRAIG STEELWORKS, 1962

STEEL
ROLLING MILL, RAVENSCRAIG STEELWORKS, 1962

STEEL
Upper
COLVILLES, CLUGSTON YARDS, 1966
Lower
COLVILLES ORE TERMINAL FROM THE SPENCE FLATS, 1964
Opposite
COLVILLES, CLUGSTON YARDS, 1966

GORBALS
Upper
GORBALS SKYLINE, 1964
Lower
FLORENCE STREET, GORBALS, 1964

GORBALS
Upper
SLEET IN CAMDEN STREET, GORBALS, 1968
Lower
GOING TO THE STEAMIE, GORBALS, 1963

GORBALS
Upper
FUNERAL PARTY AWAITING THE HEARSE, GORBALS, 1963
Lower
FLITTING, GORBALS, 1965
Opposite
"HINGIN OOT THE WINDAE", GORBALS, 1964

GORBALS
Upper
WHISKY DRAY, GORBALS, 1964
Lower
OLD MAN WITH PRAM, GORBALS, 1964

GORBALS
Upper
FRUITSELLER AT THE OLD MOY BAR, GORBALS, 1964
Lower
THE CUMBERLAND ARMS, GORBALS, 1964

GORBALS
Upper
PEND, GORBALS, 1963
Lower
LAMPLIGHTER, GORBALS, 1964

GORBALS
Upper
BOYS ON WALL, GORBALS, 1963
Lower
CHILDREN ON STREET, GORBALS, 1963

GORBALS
BACK COURT, GORBALS, 1963

GORBALS
Upper
CHILDREN, GORBALS, 1964
Lower
"GOLDEN-HAIRED LASS", GORBALS, 1964

GORBALS
Upper
BOYS AND CART, GORBALS, 1964
Lower
RAG AND BONE MAN, GORBALS, 1964

GORBALS
Upper
BOY AND PRAM, GORBALS, 1964
Lower
GIRLS AND DOG, GORBALS, 1963

GORBALS
Upper
CHILDREN IN BACK COURT, GORBALS, 1963
Lower
BOY AND BRAZIER, GORBALS, 1968
Opposite
STREET GAMES, GORBALS, 1964

GORBALS
Upper
OLD MAN, BACK COURT, GORBALS, 1963
Lower
WATCHING DEMOLITION, GORBALS, 1963

GORBALS
Upper
CUMBERLAND STREET, GORBALS, 1968
Lower
"MIRACLE OF THE GORBALS", 1964

79

GORBALS
PRAMS AND RUBBLE, GORBALS, 1963

GORBALS
Upper left
DEMOLITION WORKER, GORBALS, 1964
Upper right
DEMOLITION WORKER, GORBALS, 1964
Lower
DEMOLITION WORKERS, TEA BREAK, GORBALS, 1964

GORBALS
Upper
GORBALS WITH SOUTHERN NECROPOLIS BEYOND, 1964
Lower
ROOFTOPS AND SPENCE FLATS, GORBALS, 1963

GORBALS
Upper
SUNSET, GORBALS, 1965
Lower
THE OLD AND THE NEW, GORBALS, 1968

83

GORBALS
HUTCHESONTOWN FLATS, GORBALS, 1966

GORBALS
Upper left
STREET PLAY, GORBALS, 1984
Upper right
MAJORETTES, GORBALS, 1986
Lower
MAY QUEEN, GORBALS, 1986

THE COMMUNAL WASH-HOUSE ("THE STEAMIE"), TOWNHEAD, 1968
Upper
THE WEEKLY VISIT TO THE TOWNHEAD STEAMIE
Lower
INTERIOR VIEW: WASHING STALLS AND DRYING RACKS

THE COMMUNAL WASH-HOUSE ("THE STEAMIE"), TOWNHEAD, 1968
WOMEN AT WORK IN THE WASHING AREA

THE COMMUNAL WASH-HOUSE ("THE STEAMIE"), TOWNHEAD, 1968
Upper
WOMAN IN THE WASHING AREA
Lower
WATER BOILER AND TEMPERATURE GAUGE

THE COMMUNAL WASH-HOUSE ("THE STEAMIE"), TOWNHEAD, 1968
Upper left
FURNACEMAN AT COAL MOUND
Upper right
DRYING MACHINE OPERATOR
Lower
A FIVE-MINUTE BREAK

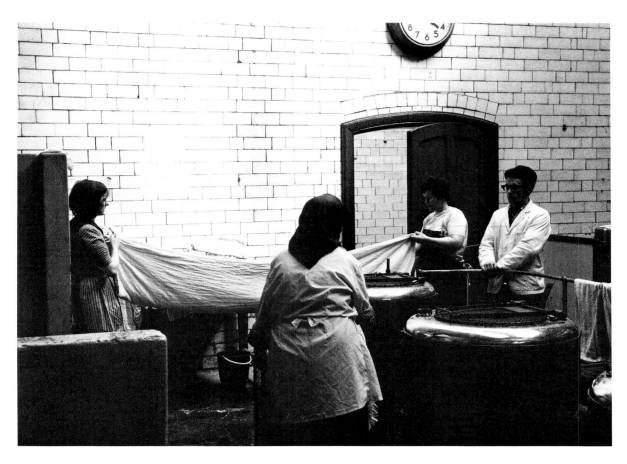

THE COMMUNAL WASH-HOUSE ("THE STEAMIE"), TOWNHEAD, 1968
Opposite
FILLING THE WASHING SACK
Upper
FOLDING BEDSHEETS
Lower
WASHING FINISHED

THE COMMUNAL WASH-HOUSE ("THE STEAMIE"), TOWNHEAD, 1968
READY FOR THE ROAD

THE COMMUNAL WASH-HOUSE ("THE STEAMIE"), TOWNHEAD, 1968
LEAVING THE STEAMIE, WITH WASHING AND SCRUBBING BOARD

MOTORWAY
Opposite
APPROACH TO KINGSTON BRIDGE DURING CONSTRUCTION, 1968
Upper left
CONSTRUCTION WORKERS, KINGSTON BRIDGE, 1968
Upper right
KINGSTON BRIDGE DURING CONSTRUCTION, 1968
Lower
TOWNHEAD INTERCHANGE DURING CONSTRUCTION, 1968

MOTORWAY
Upper
NORTH APPROACH TO THE CLYDE TUNNEL DURING CONSTRUCTION, 1968
Lower
MOTORWAY DURING CONSTRUCTION AT TOWNHEAD, JANUARY 1968

MOTORWAY
Upper
TOWNHEAD INTERCHANGE, JULY 1968
Lower
M8 MOTORWAY AT CHARING CROSS, 1985

RED ROAD FLATS/CHILDREN/DEMOLITION
RED ROAD FLATS, 1966

RED ROAD FLATS/CHILDREN/DEMOLITION
CHILDREN, ROTTENROW, 1970

RED ROAD FLATS/CHILDREN/DEMOLITION
THE CASTLEMILK LADS, 1963

RED ROAD FLATS/CHILDREN/DEMOLITION
Upper
FOOTBALL, FORTH AND CLYDE CANAL, NEAR PINKSTON, 1962
Lower
THE FOUNTAIN, CHARING CROSS BEFORE DEMOLITION, 1968

RED ROAD FLATS/CHILDREN/DEMOLITION
Upper
THE FORMER BRITISH RAIL GOODS YARD, LOOKING TOWARDS DUKE STREET, 1987
Lower
THE FORMER BRITISH RAIL GOODS YARD, HIGH STREET, LOOKING SOUTH TO REDEVELOPMENT AREA , 1987

RED ROAD FLATS/CHILDREN/DEMOLITION
Upper
DEMOLITION, CHARING CROSS, 1970
Lower
DEMOLITION, ST ENOCHS, 1978

GARNETHILL
Upper
HILL STREET, GARNETHILL, 1959
Lower
BOY IN LANE, GARNETHILL, 1964

GARNETHILL
Upper left
GARNETHILL MURAL PROJECT (1979), 1986
Upper right
TENEMENT, GARNETHILL, 1986
Lower
TIN TIN BOOKSHOP, HILL STREET, GARNETHILL, 1986

SHOPPERS/PEOPLE
HYDEPARK STREET, ANDERSTON, 1963

SHOPPERS/PEOPLE
Upper left
RAG AND BONE MAN, MARYHILL, 1956
Upper right
MAN AND PIGEONS, GEORGE SQUARE, 1964
Lower left
COOPER, VINEGARHILL, 1985
Lower right
TERRY, TATTOO ARTIST, GALLOWGATE, 1985

SHOPPERS/PEOPLE
Upper
JOHN SMITH BOOKSHOP, ST VINCENT STREET, 1962
Lower
CHILDREN, GEORGE SQUARE, 1960

SHOPPERS/PEOPLE
Upper
ARGYLE STREET, 1963
Lower
STREET PLAN, GEORGE SQUARE, 1960

SHOPPERS/PEOPLE
Upper
JAPANESE GIRLS, CHARING CROSS, 1960
Lower
PUNKS, GEORGE SQUARE, 1986

SHOPPERS/PEOPLE
THE SAMSON CHILDREN IN JOAN EARDLEY'S STUDIO, TOWNHEAD, 1962

SHOPPERS/PEOPLE
Upper
WOOLWORTHS, ARGYLE STREET, 1964
Lower
CHRISTMAS AT FRASERS, BUCHANAN STREET, 1982
Opposite
QUEENS ARCADE, COWCADDENS, 1962

SHOPPERS/PEOPLE
Upper
COBBLER, BYRES ROAD, 1974
Lower
MEWS ARCADE, RUTHVEN LANE, 1986
Opposite
GROSVENOR CAFE, CRESSWELL LANE, 1986

KELVINBRIDGE AND RAMSAY LADDERS DEPOT
Upper
RAMSAY LADDERS DEPOT, KELVINBRIDGE, 1958
Lower
KELVINBRIDGE, 1986

KELVINBRIDGE AND RAMSAY LADDERS DEPOT
Upper
COAL BAGS, KELVINBRIDGE, 1961
Lower
UNLOADING COAL FROM TRAIN, KELVINBRIDGE, 1961

KELVINBRIDGE AND RAMSAY LADDERS DEPOT
Upper
MAN AND COAL WAGONS, KELVINBRIDGE, 1961
Lower
RAMSAY LADDERS DEPOT, KELVINBRIDGE, 1961

KELVINBRIDGE AND RAMSAY LADDERS DEPOT
Upper
TEA BREAK, RAMSAY LADDERS DEPOT, KELVINBRIDGE, 1961
Lower
COAL LORRY, KELVINBRIDGE, 1961

CHRISTMAS
CHRISTMAS, CENTRAL STATION, 1964

CHRISTMAS
Upper
CHILDREN'S CHRISTMAS PARTY, PARKHEAD, 1961
Lower
CHRISTMAS LIGHTS, ARGYLE STREET, 1964

CHRISTMAS
PENSIONERS' DEMONSTRATION, GEORGE SQUARE, 1964

CHRISTMAS
CHRISTMAS AT FRASERS, BUCHANAN STREET, 1982

THE UNDERGROUND/ARGYLE LINE
TRACK LAYING, COATBRIDGE, 1966

THE UNDERGROUND/ARGYLE LINE
Upper
GLASGOW CROSS STATION, 1976
Lower
TRACK LAYING, ARGYLE LINE, 1976

THE UNDERGROUND/ARGYLE LINE
Opposite
KIOSK, ST ENOCHS UNDERGROUND STATION, 1977
Upper
UNDERGROUND WORKSHOP WORKERS, GOVAN, 1977
Lower
ST ENOCHS UNDERGROUND STATION, 1977

THE UNDERGROUND/ARGYLE LINE
Upper
TICKET INSPECTORS, ST ENOCHS UNDERGROUND STATION, 1977
Middle
STAIRS, ST ENOCHS UNDERGROUND STATION, 1977
Lower
COPLAND ROAD UNDERGROUND STATION, 1977

128

THE UNDERGROUND/ARGYLE LINE
Upper
ST ENOCHS UNDERGROUND STATION, 1985
Middle
ESCALATORS AT KELVINBRIDGE UNDERGROUND STATION, 1986
Lower
ST ENOCHS UNDERGROUND STATION, 1985

FISH AND MEAT MARKETS
Upper
ENTRANCE, MEAT MARKET, 1969.
Lower
PORTERS, MEAT MARKET, 1969.

FISH AND MEAT MARKETS
Upper
FISH MARKET, 1969.
Lower
SALESMAN, FISH MARKET, 1977.

Feelin Wabbit? Don't make a
Buy a Rabbit Cod 'o' yirsel! Warm Price!
HADD 79p
HIT 78p
LE 65p

FISH AND MEAT MARKETS
Upper
OLD FISH MARKET, 1977.
Lower
NEW BRIGGAIT CENTRE (OLD FISH MARKET), 1986.
Opposite
"THE FISH PLAICE", 1985.

THE BARROWS AND PADDY'S MARKET
Upper
STOCKINGS STALL, THE BARROWS, 1968.
Lower
THE BARROWS, 1968.

THE BARROWS AND PADDY'S MARKET
Upper
PADDY'S MARKET, 1972.
Lower left
TEA BREAK, PADDY'S MARKET, 1985.
Lower right
PADDY'S MARKET, 1986.

MODEL LODGING HOUSES
Upper
MODEL LODGING HOUSE, MARYHILL, 1971.
Middle
INTERIOR, MODEL LODGING HOUSE, MARYHILL, 1971.
Lower
CHARACTERS, PADDY'S MARKET, 1986.

POLITICAL DEMONSTRATIONS
Upper
ANTI-POLARIS MARCH, 1960
Middle
"MUST GLASGOW PERISH", ANTI-POLARIS MARCH, 1961
Lower
ANTI-POLARIS MARCH, SAUCHIEHALL STREET, 1961

POLITICAL DEMONSTRATIONS
Upper
A. J. P. TAYLOR, ST ANDREW'S HALLS, 1960
Lower
CND POSTERS,. ANTI-POLARIS MARCH, 1961
Opposite
UPPER CLYDE SHIPYARDS (UCS) PROTEST MARCH, JOHN STREET, 1971

POLITICAL DEMONSTRATIONS
Upper
MOUNTED POLICEMAN, UCS PROTEST MARCH, 1971
Lower
"WE WANT WORK" UCS PROTEST MARCH, GLASGOW GREEN, 1971

POLITICAL DEMONSTRATIONS
Upper
THE HUMBLEBUMS (BILLY CONNOLLY, LEFT) AND MATT McGINN, UCS PROTEST MARCH, GLASGOW GREEN, 1971
Lower
TONY BENN, JIMMY REID AND OTHERS, UCS PROTEST MARCH, GLASGOW GREEN, 1971

POLITICAL DEMONSTRATIONS
Opposite
RED FLAG OVER THE CITY CHAMBERS, 1985
Upper
UCS DEMONSTRATION, GLASGOW GREEN, 1971
Lower
HARRY McSHANE, WITH THE CALTON WEAVERS COMMEMORATIVE MEDAL, AFTER THE MAY DAY MARCH, GLASGOW GREEN, 1987

POLITICAL DEMONSTRATIONS
Upper
FINAL DAY OF THE WEAVERS AT W. H. HOLLINS, BRIDGETON CROSS, 1987
Lower
MAY DAY CATERPILLAR TRACTOR PROTEST, GEORGE SQUARE, 1987

RELIGIOUS DEMONSTRATIONS
Upper
PIPE BAND, BUCHANAN STREET, REMEMBRANCE SUNDAY, 1960
Lower
REMEMBRANCE SUNDAY, GEORGE SQUARE, 1960

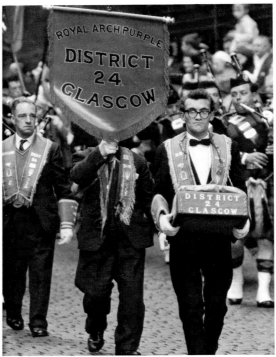

RELIGIOUS DEMONSTRATIONS
Upper left
ORANGE WALK, 1964
Upper right
ORANGE WALK, 1964
Lower
ACCORDION BAND, ORANGE WALK, 1964

146

RELIGIOUS DEMONSTRATIONS
Upper
POPEMOBILE, POPE JOHN PAUL II'S VISIT TO SCOTLAND, BELLAHOUSTON PARK, 1982
Middle
PODIUM, POPE JOHN PAUL II'S VISIT TO SCOTLAND, BELLAHOUSTON PARK, 1982
Lower
CROWD, POPE JOHN PAUL II'S VISIT TO SCOTLAND, BELLAHOUSTON PARK, 1982

PARKS
SUN AND TREES, KELVINGROVE PARK, 1959

PARKS
Upper
KELVINGROVE PARK, 1963
Lower
SLEDGING, KELVINGROVE PARK, 1966

149

PARKS
Upper
MISS SCOTLAND, THE FOUNTAIN, KELVINGROVE PARK, 1963
Lower
PARK BENCH, GLASGOW GREEN, 1966

PARKS
Upper
LOVERS, BOTANIC GARDENS, 1967
Lower
KIBBLE PALACE, BOTANIC GARDENS, 1986

SPORT
Upper
CUP FINAL, HAMPDEN PARK, 1963
Lower
CROWD, CUP FINAL, HAMPDEN PARK, 1963

SPORT
Upper
CUP FINAL, HAMPDEN PARK, 1963
Lower
CELTIC END, CUP FINAL, HAMPDEN PARK, 1963

SPORT
Upper
JOCK STEIN AND CELTIC TEAM, TACTICS ROOM, PARKHEAD, 1967
Lower
PARADING THE EUROPEAN CUP, CELTIC PARK, PARKHEAD, 1967

SPORT
Upper
IBROX PARK, RANGERS FOOTBALL STADIUM, 1987
Lower
GRAEME SOUNESS SIGNING AUTOGRAPHS, IBROX PARK, 1987

SPORT
Upper
START OF WOMEN'S MINI MARATHON, INDIA STREET, 1983
Lower
WOMEN'S MINI MARATHON, INDIA STREET CAR PARK, 1984

SPORT
Upper
MARATHON, GLASGOW CROSS, 1983
Lower
MARATHON FINISHING STRAIGHT, GLASGOW GREEN, 1983

SPORT
Upper
MONTE CARLO RALLY START, BLYTHSWOOD SQUARE, 1964
Lower
AEROBICS, CLYDE WALKWAY, 1984

SPORT
Upper
SILVER BROOM WORLD CHAMPIONSHIP CURLING, KELVIN HALL, 1985
Lower
OPENING DAY, CROWN POINT SPORTS PARK, 1985

CARNIVALS/SHOWS
Upper
DAIRY SHOW, KELVIN HALL, 1962
Lower
DAIRY SHOW, KELVIN HALL, 1962

CARNIVALS/SHOWS
Upper left
DOG SHOW, KELVIN HALL, 1960
Upper right
CARNIVAL AT GLASGOW GREEN, 1963
Lower
ROUNDABOUT, CARNIVAL, GLASGOW GREEN, 1964

SPECIAL EVENTS
Upper
CROWD, QUEEN MOTHER'S VISIT TO TRANSPORT MUSEUM, ALBERT DRIVE, 1963
Lower
QUEEN MOTHER AT THE TRANSPORT MUSEUM, ALBERT DRIVE, 1963
Opposite
CARNIVAL, GLASGOW GREEN, 1963

SPECIAL EVENTS
Upper
STUDENTS CHARITY RAG, 1961.
Lower
CHILDREN'S ANNUAL TAXI RUN, KELVIN WAY, 1986.

SPECIAL EVENTS
Upper
HIGHLAND DANCING, WORLD PIPE BAND CHAMPIONSHIPS, BELLAHOUSTON PARK, 1984.
Lower
TUNING UP, WORLD PIPE BAND CHAMPIONSHIPS, BELLAHOUSTON PARK, 1986.

ENTERTAINMENT
BARROWLAND BALLROOM, 1963

ENTERTAINMENT
Upper
THÉRON'S FASHION SHOW, McLELLAN GALLERIES, 1961
Lower
THÉRON'S FASHION SHOW, McLELLAN GALLERIES, 1961

ENTERTAINMENT
Upper
H.L.I. BAR, MARYHILL ROAD, 1964
Lower
KING'S ARMS, BATH STREET, 1968

ENTERTAINMENT
Upper
BERLIN BAR, GEORGE SQUARE, 1986
Lower
THE WAREHOUSE DISCO, 1983

EDUCATION
Upper
ADELPHI NURSERY SCHOOL, GORBALS, 1987
Lower
FIRST COMMUNION DAY, ST BRIDGET'S, BAILLIESTON, 1978

170

EDUCATION
Upper
ST MARK'S PRIMARY, SHETTLESTON, 1962
Lower
ART CLASS, ST MARK'S PRIMARY, SHETTLESTON, 1962

EDUCATION
Upper
ART CLASS AT RECENTLY OPENED EASTBANK ACADEMY, 1987
Lower
SCIENCE CLASS AT RECENTLY OPENED EASTBANK ACADEMY, 1987

EDUCATION
Upper
GRADUATION, GLASGOW UNIVERSITY, 1982
Lower
DEGREE SHOWS, GLASGOW SCHOOL OF ART, 1987

ARTS
PAINTINGS FOR SALE, BOTANIC GARDENS, 1958
Opposite
BURRELL GALLERY, POLLOK PARK, 1986

ARTS
Upper
J. D. FERGUSSON AND DONALD BAIN, McLELLAN GALLERIES, 1959
Lower
JOAN EARDLEY IN HER TOWNHEAD STUDIO, 1962

ARTS
ALASDAIR GRAY, 1960

ARTS
Upper
"THE REALIST TRADITION" EXHIBITION, GLASGOW ART GALLERY AND MUSEUM, KELVINGROVE, 1981
Lower
GLASGOW ART GALLERY AND MUSEUM, KELVINGROVE, 1981

ARTS
Upper
JOHN TAYLOR EXHIBITION, THIRD EYE CENTRE, 1982
Lower
PROJECT ABILITY, THIRD EYE CENTRE, 1983

ARTS
KATE THOMSON, ARTIST IN RESIDENCE, GORBALS FAIR SOCIETY; MURAL PAINTING AT THE ADELPHI NURSERY SCHOOL, 1987

ARTS
DEGREE SHOW, SCULPTURE SCHOOL, GLASGOW SCHOOL OF ART, 1987

ARTS
Upper
MURAL PAINTING AT THE ADELPHI NURSERY SCHOOL, 1987
Lower
VISUAL ARTS WORKSHOP EXHIBITION, GORBALS FAIR SOCIETY, 1986.

ARTS
Upper
POLLOK HOUSE, POLLOK PARK, 1986
Lower
PEOPLE'S PALACE, GLASGOW GREEN, 1986

ARTS
Upper
FOYER, JIMMY LOGAN'S METROPOLE THEATRE, 1965
Lower
MAURICE RÖEVES DIRECTING, CITIZENS' THEATRE, 1960s

ARTS
Upper
CLYDE FAIR AT THE OLD FRUITMARKET, 1973
Lower
CLYDE FAIR AT THE OLD FRUITMARKET, 1973

ARTS
Upper left
PAVEMENT ARTIST, SAUCHIEHALL STREET, 1984
Upper right
MAYFEST, GEORGE SQUARE, 1986
Lower
PENNY GEGGIES, BUCHANAN STREET, 1982

ARTS
Upper
EDWIN MORGAN, "SONNETS FROM SCOTLAND" BOOKSIGNING, THIRD EYE CENTRE, 1986
Lower
BILL FORSYTH AND CLARE GROGAN DURING FILMING OF "COMFORT AND JOY", GLASGOW, 1983

ARTS
Upper
"SUGAR 'N' SPITE", LIZ LOCHHEAD, SIOBHAN REDMOND, ESTHER ALLAN, TRON THEATRE, 1982
Lower
MARCELLA EVARISTI AND ELAINE COLLINS, "TERRESTRIAL EXTRAS", TRON THEATRE, MAYFEST, 1986

ARTS
"THE STEAMIE" AT GOVAN STEAMIE, MAYFEST 1987. WILDCAT STAGE PRODUCTION (L. TO R. IDA SCHUSTER, RAY JEFFRIES, ELAINE C. SMITH, KATY MURPHY, DOROTHY PAUL)

ARTS
Upper left
DANCERS OF THE CELTIC BALLET, 1961
Upper right
GLASGOW THEATRE BALLET, REHEARSAL STUDIOS, 1968
Lower
"ROMEO AND JULIET", SCOTTISH BALLET, THEATRE ROYAL, 1982

190

ARTS
Upper
"L'EGISTO", SCOTTISH OPERA, THEATRE ROYAL, 1982
Lower
DEACON BLUE IN CONCERT, THE PAVILION, 1987

ARTS
SIR ALEXANDER GIBSON, "LAST NIGHT AT THE PROMS", KELVIN HALL, 1982
Lower
CANTILENA, HENRY WOOD HALL, 1985

ARTS
Upper
ALLY BAIN IN CONCERT, BABBITY BOWSTER, 1986
Lower
CEILIDH WITH THE GALLIVANTERS AT THE WINTER GARDEN, PEOPLE'S PALACE, MAYFEST, 1987

193

ARTS
GEORGE WYLLIE AND "THE STRAW LOCOMOTIVE", MAYFEST, 1987

GLASGOW WELCOMES

NEW GLASGOW
CITY CHAMBERS, GEORGE SQUARE, 1985

NEW GLASGOW
Upper
QUEEN STREET STATION, 1984
Lower
JAMAICA STREET, 1984

NEW GLASGOW
Upper
CLYDESDALE BANK, BUCHANAN STREET, 1983
Lower
BANK OF SCOTLAND, QUEEN STREET, 1981

NEW GLASGOW
Upper
ANDERSTON FLATS, 1985
Lower
BRITOIL BUILDING, ST VINCENT STREET, 1985

NEW GLASGOW
Upper
MOSQUE, CLYDESIDE, 1981
Lower
NEW SHERIFF COURT, 1986

NEW GLASGOW
Upper
BOOTS BUILDING, SAUCHIEHALL STREET, 1982
Lower
WOODSIDE INN, MARYHILL ROAD, 1982

200

NEW GLASGOW
Upper
PEDESTRIAN PRECINCT, SAUCHIEHALL STREET, 1984
Lower
ST ENOCHS SQUARE, 1981

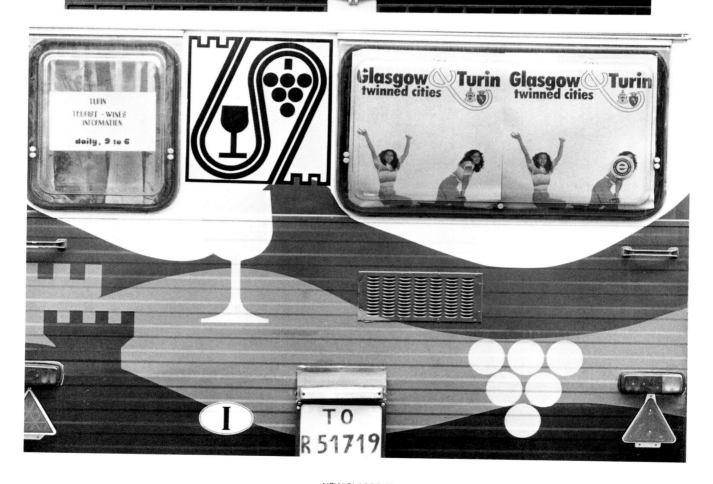

NEW GLASGOW
Upper
THE WAREHOUSE, GLASSFORD STREET, 1985
Lower
GLASGOW-TURIN TWINNING, 1982

NEW GLASGOW
Upper
CAFÉ, PEOPLE'S PALACE, GLASGOW GREEN, 1986
Lower
GLASGOW UNIVERSITY AND SCOTTISH EXHIBITION AND CONFERENCE CENTRE, FROM THE SITE OF THE 1988 GARDEN FESTIVAL, 1987

NEW GLASGOW
Upper
TEMPLETON BUSINESS CENTRE, OFF GLASGOW GREEN, 1987

Lower
BUCHANAN STREET PEDESTRIAN PRECINCT IN WINTER, 1982

Opposite
TRINITY COLLEGE TOWERS FROM SCOTTISH EXHIBITION AND CONFERENCE CENTRE, 1986

Notes by

JOE FISHER

with

CORDELIA OLIVER

on the Arts

A short commentary on the photographs
of OSCAR MARZAROLI

CITYSCAPES

It is difficult to get to grips with the urban landscape of Glasgow. Edinburgh flaunts her charms, saying, "Regard me, am I not beautiful!"; although shyness is not a usual attribute of our city, her architectural attractions are somewhat elusive, fleeting and accidental, but nevertheless visible to the discerning eye; and increasingly so as stone-cleaning removes layers of industrial grime, and the beauty of much of its surviving Victorian architecture is revealed.

Much has been lost through her attitude, utilitarian not to say Gradgrindian, of "Not needed, knock down!", but nevertheless her 13th-century cathedral still rises from its surrounding clutter, although its neighbour, the cupola'd Royal Infirmary, is a poor replacement for its predecessor, a classic Adam building. While the fantastic and grandiose Art Gallery building (1892-1900) confronts the University of Glasgow across the airy valley of the wooded Kelvingrove, Charles Rennie Mackintosh's masterpiece, the austere Glasgow School of Art (1897-1909), fights its way out of a huddle of nondescript roofs. The Park Circus area came into being between 1830 and 1870. Built to house the city's professional and business aristocracy it is now given over to offices, clubs, consulates, schools and studios. Its skyline is still, miraculously, intact — one of the most exciting the city has to offer.

Other aspects of the city's past have also disappeared. At one time the Kelvin, as it flowed past Partick, drove many mills — paper, flint, snuff, wheat and barley — but the very last of them, the Regent Flour Mill, no longer perches on its east bank below Dumbarton bridge.

Glasgow's layout has been strongly influenced by its physical setting, by the river with its many bridges, road and rail, which stitch together the city's north and south sides, by its uncounted drumlins, glacial mounds of clayey soil, seen here rushing vertiginously down to Sir Walter Scott, aloft on his column in George Square.

THE CLYDE/SHIPBUILDING

Once our city proudly boasted that "Glasgow made the Clyde and the Clyde made Glasgow", reference to the laborious conversion during the 18th and 19th centuries of a shallow unnavigable stream into a deep channel down which sea-going Clyde-built ships could make their way to the world's oceans. On its north bank the Stobcross hammerhead crane, 175 feet high, is a mute reminder of the river's past glory, while the P.S. *Waverley* is the last witness of the fleets of Clyde paddle steamers with their multicoloured funnels which once raced each other "doon the watter" to the flourishing Clyde resorts of Dunoon, Rothesay, Largs, Millport, Helensburgh, Campbeltown and beyond. Even the six-vessel fleet of little ferries which braved the debris-laden waters of the city river disappeared off its face in 1977.

STEEL

The discovery near Glasgow at the beginning of last century of abundant sources of coal and iron ore turned the city into the workshop of the Empire, producing locomotives, cranes, bridges and all sorts of heavy engineering. When the local iron ore gave out, the intricate tangle of giant cranes at the General Terminus Quay, first opened on the south bank of the river in 1849, enabled ship-borne foreign ore to be unloaded in the centre of the city.

GORBALS

Once a tiny community clustered about the south end of the old Glasgow bridge, then a high-class residential district planned and laid-out by the Laurie brothers, still later a centre of Glasgow's Jewry, by the end of the 19th century the Gorbals had become one of the most "tenemented" areas of the city. Resistless change has removed most of this Gorbals along with the way of life it bred — the hundreds of small shops and street-corner barrows which supplied the tenement-dwellers with their daily needs of both provisions and local news, the "steamies" or communal wash-houses, visited daily by countless superannuated prams piled high with household washing, the expressions of religious beliefs encoded in enigmatic graffiti, "Rangers for the Cup and League, F.T.P." — all gone, leaving nothing behind but the whisper of dusty wind between high-rise tower blocks.

THE COMMUNAL WASH-HOUSE

An early and strong believer in municipal socialism, the old Glasgow Corporation supplied its citizens with gas, electricity, houses, water and transport. The concomitants of an industrial metropolis, smoke, smut and other air-borne impurities, along with "drying greens" given over to mud, dogs and children, made household washing (and drying) almost impossible, so the Corporation in its paternalism set up a series of communal washhouses (commonly known as "steamies"). Thriftily, these were usually associated with public baths so that the one boiler served both purposes. To these steamies, almost daily, the tenement housewives trundled their washing in a variety of conveyances, mainly broken-down prams and go-chairs; the élite had custom-built bogies with little noisy iron wheels. Here the family's clothes could be washed and dried with the aid of huge sinks, abundant hot water, giant spin-driers and long drying racks which pulled out from the wall. This was very much a woman's world; the language and topics would have brought a blush to the face of a Glasgow "polisman", hence the phrase used to describe some piece of particularly scabrous gossip — "the talk of the steamie".

MOTORWAY

In a city where the average number of car owners lagged considerably behind the nation as a whole, the destruction of entire living areas of Glasgow, like Townhead and the Cowcaddens, in order to run concrete rivers through deserts of red blaes generated a great deal of adverse criticism. The incoherence of the unconnected bits of preliminary construction, shown graphically in these photographs, gave no indication of the final plan, and all the criticism seemed justified.

And yet it is difficult to stand, say, at Charing Cross and watch the dusk-rush of glowworm car lights down the deep trench leading to the Kingston Bridge and not to wonder how our horse-and-cart roads could ever have coped with such traffic flows.

By day, Charing Cross presents another aspect, for the thoughtful planting of native trees and shrubs has created a unified organic landscape which softens and offsets the cityscape around them.

Had these colossal works been dug out of the shifting sands of North Africa, how we would have praised the Roman engineers for their daring, ingenuity and foresight!

RED ROAD FLATS/CHILDREN/DEMOLITION

Excellent reminders of the once ubiquitous Gospel according to Le Corbusier, these flats, higher than St Paul's and the tallest council flats in Europe, have not escaped their share of the criticism now being levelled at this high-rise way of life. From old folk marooned on the twentieth floor to coffins propped upright in the narrow lifts, from pieces of masonry accelerating downwards at thirty-two feet per second per second to vandals doing the same in the lift shafts, their characteristics have in no way endeared them to anyone except, possibly, the architects. Nowadays, in providing accommodation for students and nurses, some amends are being made.

The cooling tower of Pinkston Power Station, which produced the electricity which drove the city's tramcars, supplies a backdrop to the cobblestone street playground on the edge of the Forth and Clyde canal. The cooling tower is no more but the canal, a relic of a much earlier era of transport, still winds its tortuous way through Maryhill and Port Dundas.

The terracotta monument to Sir Charles Cameron, a long-forgotten Glasgow MP, now droops uneasily and alone above the sunken ring-road at Charing Cross — but for the magnificent range of the Charing Cross Mansions all else visible in this photograph has disappeared.

St Enoch Railway Station, completed in 1880, served as the terminus of the south-west of Scotland railway system. After a short eighty-six years of activity, its massive towering structure has completely disappeared, both the station and its hotel, and a glass and metal shopping centre is rising in their place.

GARNETHILL

Perched high on one of the city's many drumlins and lying to the north of Sauchiehall Street, Garnethill began as a high-class residential district. Later it became known as an area of theatrical digs, and now is an Oriental enclave where the schools carry notices in Chinese ideographs and the Bank of China offers its services.

It also has several good examples of an art form extensively used in Glasgow — gable-end paintings, many of which manage to combine graphic art, wit and poetry. It also has a tiny church building which began, before the First World War, as German Lutheran, continued as Free Presbyterian and is now Tridentine Catholic!

The home of Glasgow School of Art, housed in various buildings on the hillside, Garnethill has always reflected Glasgow's bohemian and cosmopolitan interests.

SHOPPERS/PEOPLE

John Smith & Son proudly claim (from premises about six times as high as they are broad) a bookselling existence going back all the way to 1751, in the heyday of the city's Tobacco Lords.

At one time Glasgow offered a multiplicity of arcades to its shoppers — Wellington, Queen's, Royal, Millar's. Their undercover shopping facilities, reminiscent of the city's earlier shop-lined piazzas, are now only a disappearing memory. One remains, the Argyle Arcade, where brightly lit shop windows gleaming with engagement rings and quartz watches dazzle the passers-by.

"Girring a boin" will still produce the iron-banded wooden tub so proudly displayed by this Glasgow cooper. His craft, one of the fourteen Incorporated Trades of the city, once provided the many containers for a wide range of solids and liquids from tobacco to milk. Now even the beer is delivered in steel or plastic barrels!

The opulent upmarket splendour of a Buchanan Street store contrasts vividly with the indiscriminate and homely clutter of an old-time Woolworth's counter, unpackaged biscuits and all.

It has been said that it was in her paintings of Glasgow children that Joan Eardley displayed her talents at their fullest powers. This candid photograph of a group of such children — the Samson family — immortalised by her in many paintings and drawings, enables us to realise how a true artist can both show us with accuracy the visible world and also create a work of art.

Page 116

KELVINBRIDGE AND RAMSAY LADDERS DEPOT

The twists and turns of a river's passage through a city often isolate small level patches, unused for residential purposes and often given over to industrial uses. The little triangle of flood-plain south of the Kelvin Bridge on the Great Western Road used to be occupied by Kelvinbridge Railway Station (c. 1894) on the vanished Kirklee Line. Although its passenger service closed down in 1952 it still continued as a mineral yard (or in more mundane words, a coal ree) and as a store for a manufacturer of ladders. The ladder firm was based in Forfar, only maintaining a depot in Glasgow, hence the slightly ambiguous title of "Ramsay Ladders Depot".

Page 120

CHRISTMAS

Fifty or so years ago, Glasgow children were quite used to their fathers going off to work as usual even though it was Christmas Day. For centuries a festival studiously ignored by the Scottish kirk, it really only came into its own after the Second World War when one of the signs of peace was the blacked-out windows giving place to displays of multicoloured Christmas tree lights.

Page 124

THE UNDERGROUND/ARGYLE LINE

It is quite possible for someone born and bred in Glasgow to reach adulthood without ever having set foot in the city's minuscule underground system. This may explain why it occupies a somewhat ambiguous position, praised and vigorously defended by the few and unknown or ignored by the many. It opened in 1896 at a cost of £1.5 million, and after almost forty years of pulling its little toy-town carriages round its six-and-a-half miles of track by means of an endless rope, it was converted to electric traction. Eventually these creaking carriages celebrated their eightieth birthday, still in everyday use, but shortly after this the entire system was somewhat expensively dragged into the 20th century. In 1979 the Queen opened what the soon became known as "The Clockwork Orange" and once more Tradeston, Kinning Park and the Gorbals could communicate freely with Hillhead, Kelvinbridge and the Cowcaddens.

FISH AND MEAT MARKETS

In mediaeval times the lucrative right of a community to hold its own market was eagerly sought, and Glasgow's market goes all the way back to the late 12th century. Over the centuries this general market began to subdivide until by the early 19th century our citizens could make use of a whole series of specialist markets — cheese, poultry, old clothes, fish, birds and dogs, dead meat, cattle and horses, butter, fruit and vegetables.

The Meat Market, located in the old days near the north end of the old Glasgow Bridge (to the intense annoyance of the residents), was moved in 1818 to an area lying south of Duke Street, in the east end of the city. At its busiest this market could accommodate 2,000 cattle and 15,000 sheep and for more than a century and a half it has helped to fill the insatiable maw of a large carnivorous community.

A Fish Market has existed in various sites in the city, no doubt ever since the first fish was taken from the Clyde. The market's last central city site was, appropriately, only a stone's throw from the river, located in the Bridgegate, where a French Renaissance-style building was opened in 1873. After the market moved out to Blochairn in 1977 to join the similarly exiled Fruit Market, the deserted building lay empty for a while but it is now up and going as the £1.5 million shop and leisure Briggait Centre.

PADDY'S MARKET

We first hear of a Glasgow Clothes Market back in the 1850s. It enjoyed an eventful life, moving from Jail Square to the old City Slaughterhouse, then transferring in the 1870s to Greendyke Street on the north side of Glasgow Green, being taken over by the Corporation at the end of the century and finally closing down shortly after the end of the First World War. Parallel to it, however, developed another somewhat different clothes market, one whose customers found that even the established market was too expensive for them. The position of the Highland immigrant at the bottom of the social pyramid was taken over in the first half of the 19th century by the Irish immigrant, and when an *alfresco* old clothes market started up in Great Clyde Street, it was well-nigh inevitable that it should be given the name "Paddy's Market". Between the wars it moved into a cul-de-sac off Shipbank Lane, up against the massive wall of the railway viaduct leading into the now-vanished St Enoch Station. There it still leads a vigorous but precarious life, constantly under threat of official extinction.

THE BARROWS

The street market popularly called the Barrows (no need to indulge in the reverse-gentrification of "The Barras") owes its existence to the growing habit of early hawkers and their loaded barrows congregating in particular areas of the central city. One of the most popular of these areas was off the Gallowgate, near Kent Street, and the growth of its popularity was such that in 1926 part of it was covered in, although a large section was, for a long time, still left open to the weather. The majority of the stalls, particularly those under cover, have always been given over to the sale of secondhand clothes, but another useful function once performed by the Barrows was the carrying on of a considerable trade in hand tools of all kinds. Every Saturday afternoon the alleys between the open stalls were thronged with working men in the ubiquitous cloth caps and mufflers fingering chisels and springing saws.

It is said that nowadays during any weekend 500 to 1,000 stalls flourish there and that it is the largest covered market in Europe. It is now run by the Barras Enterprise, and no doubt will soon achieve the supreme accolade of becoming a stop on a Heritage Trail — poor Barrows!

Page 136

MODEL LODGING HOUSES

When the worst of Glasgow's notorious slums, which festered up and down the High Street, the Saltmarket and their closes and vennels, were cleared away under the terms of the City Improvement Trust of 1866, the Town Council found itself obliged to make provision for the housing of the many inmates of those private common lodging houses which had been destroyed in the general clearance. So, between 1870 and 1878, the Council built and opened seven model lodging houses. It gives pause to think when we open today's telephone directory and, under Glasgow District Council, Hotel and Lodging House Accommodation, find *nine* addresses.

Page 137

POLITICAL DEMONSTRATIONS

Look at those faces, those banners, those crowds — ought we to wonder where the "perfervid" enthusiasm which animated them has gone? One survivor at least remains — Harry McShane. Born in 1892, and the last of the "Red Clydesiders", Harry McShane is a Scottish Marxist and was an early colleague of John Maclean. A front rank member of the Communist Party (from which he resigned in 1953), he has been throughout his long life a pillar of the Scottish radical left.

Professor Checkland called Glasgow an Upas tree. That fabled growth was reputed to kill everything in, above and under its branches; the local combination of inventive genius, iron ore and coal made our city so dependent on the resulting heavy engineering that nothing else has been able to thrive alongside it. The respite of two world wars delayed the inevitable but the post-war shipping glut brought our shipyards to their knees. The expectation and hopes of all those bonny fighters who walked and argued and sang and talked to try and save names and skills known across the world's oceans are all summed up in the simple plea of the banner in one of these photographs — "We Want Work".

Page 145

RELIGIOUS DEMONSTRATIONS

"The expense of spirit in a waste of shame" — the young man's face says it all, how the irresistible power of a self-sustaining myth, whose origins are scarcely apprehended by its followers, can call out unquestioning allegiance and devotion which exactly mirror the orthodoxy they set themselves against.

Who would have ever thought that a city whose motto proudly sets out the touchstone of the Protestant faith — "by the preaching of Thy Word" — could have mustered its largest-ever crowd to welcome the Bishop of Rome? Perhaps the credit for this happy meeting of opposites should be shared between the warmth of Celtic Glasgow and the charisma of John Paul.

"Lest we forget" — once the pulse of the whole city slackened and stopped every November for two long minutes. Children in their classes, housewives at home, carters and their horses, tram drivers and their trams, everyone stopped and thought —

something. Now, only at one of the most beautiful war memorials, the Cenotaph in George Square, does official Glasgow remember its dead. (By the way, who was "himslef"?)

Page 148

PARKS

It may appear strange to us now, but one of the attractive features of the private burying grounds which began to burgeon in most of our big 19th-century cities was that they afforded the working classes the opportunity of taking their recreation in green surroundings. Glasgow has always been fortunate in the access its citizens have had to less unusual open spaces, however. The first and best known of these is undoubtedly the centuries-old Glasgow Green on the north bank of the Clyde. This "Dear Green Place" has always been dear to all classes of Glaswegians and many legal battles have been fought to keep it inviolate. For instance, in 1823 attempts to mine coal from under it were foiled as was a later attempt, in 1847, to run a railway viaduct across it. Of the city's more recent parks, the oldest is the West End Park (better known nowadays by its original name of the Kelvingrove Park), bought by the Town Council in 1853 and laid out by the famous Sir Joseph Paxton of Crystal Palace fame. Over the years the Council added others — Queen's Park in 1862, Alexandra Park in 1870, Cathkin in 1886 and Bellahouston, Ruchill, Maxwell, Tollcross, Springburn and the Botanic Gardens during the 1890s; Victoria, Whiteinch and Elder Park became Glasgow parks when the city's boundaries were extended.

The inauguration of the city's Loch Katrine water supply in 1859 was commemorated in 1871 by the erection in Kelvingrove Park of an elaborate fountain in honour of Lord Provost Robert Stewart, to whose exertions the success of the project owed much. It is an endearing Victorian whigmaleerie which incorporates a most attractive series of astrological enamelled plaques. Disgracefully vandalised and bone-dry, its revitalisation is much to be looked for.

John Kibble, a Paisley engineer, of Coulport House on Loch Long, sold his huge circular conservatory to the Botanic Gardens in 1871. Popularly known as the Kibble Palace, its unencumbered internal space served as an auditorium for many famous visiting speakers. When the Americans Moody and Sankey visited our city they evangelised a crowd of over 7,000 Glasgow sinners under its glass dome, and both Gladstone and Disraeli made use of it when they were Lord Rectors of Glasgow University.

Page 152

SPORT

Glasgow has many peculiarities but none more so than the Old Firm game, for in what other city could football symbolise at a popular level the complicated differences between two types of Christianity. The "Scarlet Woman of Babylon" has been, to mix a metaphor, an age-old bogeyman of Protestant Scotland and the influx into Glasgow of large numbers of Irish during the 19th century only served to emphasise their mutual antipathies. For historic reasons two football teams quickly became identified with Protestantism and Roman Catholicsm respectively. Celtic (1888) owes its origins to the efforts of two priests in the city's east end to provide some form of recreation for their young men. Rangers' supporters did not at first obviously "kick with the right foot", but popular belief has it that the arrival in Govan of the Northern Ireland shipbuilding firm of Harland and Wolff, with a workforce which contained many

214

Orange adherents, marked the polarisation of the two teams and the beginnings of the Old Firm troubles.

The visible contrasts between the 1960s Hampden crowds and their counterparts of twenty years later tell their own story — on the one hand cloth caps and receding hairlines, not a banner in sight, scarcely a scarf, on the other jeans, trainers, scarves and a considerable drop in age levels.

How surprised the 360-year-old Tolbooth Steeple must be at seeing some 14,000 people running 26 miles 385 yards for no apparent reason — almost as surprised as to find people being publicly urged to buy such a staple food as oats!

If you look at a large-scale map of suburban 19th-century Glasgow, you will be struck by the prevalence of little curling ponds. Were the winters of these days really so cold as to guarantee a regular supply of frozen surfaces for the devotees of the roarin' game? Nowadays we decadent descendants prefer artificial ice and indoor comforts.

Page 160

CARNIVALS/SHOWS

The Glasgow Fair, by origin an annual summer market, had become by the late 17th century a sort of Glasgow Mardi Gras. During the Fair the west edge of the Glasgow Green facing the Justiciary Buildings became a yearly rendezvous for a multitude of small temporary theatres, animal shows, clowns and tightrope walkers, and the reappearance on the Green of popular entertainments is a welcome return of an old custom.

If the Green represented outdoor entertainment then the Kelvin Hall was without doubt the time-honoured venue for indoor festivites. No Glasgow child's Christmas was complete without an annual visit to the circus and shows at the Kelvin Hall, and its hospitable interior welcomed every kind of event from horse shows to dog shows, from fashions to ideal homes.

Page 163

SPECIAL EVENTS

Every community invents odd events which develop into traditions, and two of Glasgow's exhibit in outward form the essential warmth of the city. Every year the city's taxi-drivers dress up their drab-coloured vehicles with balloons and streamers and in a long procession drive through and out of the city to some seaside resort carrying in their cabs as many of the city's disadvantaged children as they can hold for a day of festivity and pleasure. Similarly, in a tradition going back to when Glasgow University's bedizened students invaded the city's streets, offices, shops and tramcars collecting in aid of the city's pre-NHS hospitals. The very best days of each winter are still brightened by flocks of amateur pirates, skeletons and ghosts shaking collecting cans under the noses of willing citizens.

Our city's warmth is wide enough to embrace all sorts and conditions of visitors. From the red-faced, huffing and puffing bagpipe competitors in the World Championships to the gracious figure of the Queen Mother opening the Museum of Transport, the city says to everyone, "Come ben the room and sit ye doon!".

ENTERTAINMENT

Our cityscapes, our older buildings and streets, still carry the marks and signs of their local origins; they belong here, they are part of the matrix out of which our community has developed. How different when we move indoors, for here we find ourselves in an anonymous dislocated world. The names may be a mixture of local and non-local — Barrowland, Berlin Bar, King's Arms, Tréron's — but the décor, the style, tell us nothing about the community into which they have been thrust.

EDUCATION

Glasgow children seem little affected by changing educational styles and we can be sure the little ones of twenty years ago, marching in regimental steps between ranked desks, were quite as happy in their own way as today's informally peripatetic pupils and their scattered work tables.

At the other end of Glasgow's educational spectrum, our two universities share between them the best of tradition and innovation — Glasgow University, established by papal bull in the 15th century, and Strathclyde University, the cumulation and extension of Glasgow's 19th-century pursuit of technical excellence. Both ceremoniously admit new graduates by the old Scottish university custom of "capping", after which there follows *en plain air* a more recent ceremony by which fond parents immortalise their tertiary offspring's achievements.

ARTS

PAINTINGS FOR SALE, BOTANIC GARDENS, 1958

In the days before publicly subsidised and commercial art galleries began to proliferate in Glasgow, with art journalists eager to assist their favourites to fame and fortune, Glasgow artists were forced to be their own selling agents. The railings of the Botanic Gardens were put to good use by painters like Tom Macdonald, Bet Low, and J. M. McChlery, whose work is seen in this photograph. Viewers at this open-air exhibition came in all sorts, from the *cognoscenti* to the casual passer-by. The photograph of the Burrell Gallery, on the opposite page, emphasises how the arts (both in practice and provision) have flourished in the intervening years.

BURRELL GALLERY, POLLOK PARK, 1986

The collection of paintings and sculpture, tapestries, art objects and antiquities, gifted to his fellow citizens by the late Sir William Burrell, took more than thirty years to find a permanent home, but Glasgow may well be proud of the Burrell Gallery, which was finally opened in 1983 in the idyllic surroundings of Pollok Park. A discreet, well-proportioned structure of glass and pink sandstone, it has been designed by Barry Gasson to enhance as well as to display a collection which is said to be the finest of its kind in Britain, outside the Victoria and Albert Museum.

J. D. FERGUSSON AND DONALD BAIN, McLELLAN GALLERIES, 1959

An historic photograph of a conversation between two painters — master and pupil in effect — at the memorial exhibiton, in the McLellan Galleries, to Alan Fletcher.

Fletcher was a young Glasgow painter of exceptional promise whose career was cut short by a fatal accident in Italy in 1959.

JOAN EARDLEY IN HER TOWNHEAD STUDIO, 1962

Joan Eardley, who died in 1963 at the age of forty-two, was one of the finest painters in the history of Scottish art. Her working life was divided between town and country, with bases in this studio in Glasgow's Townhead and in a clifftop cottage in the Kincardineshire fishing village of Catterline. Her Glasgow studio, a small eyrie with a glazed wall and roof, formerly used by generations of photographers, became the focus of years of activity when Eardley drew and painted the street urchins in a ramshackle environment which was a figurative painter's paradise, but which has now disappeared under the bulldozers.

ALASDAIR GRAY, 1960

A man of great imaginative gifts, Alasdair Gray has encapsulated his own youthful development in Glasgow's bohemian milieu in his impressive novel, *Lanark*. But his training was in the visual arts, as a student of painting at Glasgow School of Art during the 1950s and, as seen here, his talent for mural painting was given full rein. Oscar Marzaroli has caught Alasdair in a typically quizzical moment of pause while at work on a mural in the West End home of a Glasgow cinema owner.

"THE REALIST TRADITION" EXHIBITION, GLASGOW ART GALLERY AND MUSEUM, KELVINGROVE, 1981

The group of painters, the Glasgow Boys, who brought the city to wider attention at the end of last century, based their work, to a great extent, on the French Realist tradition, of which painters like Courbet, Manet and Degas were the masters, and Bastien Lepage, Bonvin, Ribot, etc., the notable runners-up. *The Realist Tradition* which came to Glasgow Art Gallery from Cleveland, USA, was, therefore, a very great attraction to the city's art lovers.

GLASGOW ART GALLERY AND MUSEUM, KELVINGROVE, 1987

Opened in 1901, and built (at a cost of £250,000) largely from the profits of the International Exhibition held in Kelvingrove Park in 1888, Glasgow's principal municipal art gallery and museum presents a typically 19th-century wedding cake vision of Renaissance architecture. It does, however, boast a few elements nearer to the then modern movement of art nouveau — in the large copper-and-glass chandeliers in the central hall with its great pipe organ and marble floor. The municipal art collection contained in the gallery is arguably the finest of any city in Britain.

JOHN TAYLOR EXHIBITION, THIRD EYE CENTRE, 1982

Third Eye Centre provides Glasgow with excellent space for showing contemporary art. Exhibitions — each with its preview attended by a wide range of enthusiasts — span the whole spectrum, from international avant garde painting and sculpture to displays of ethnic craftwork.

Some of the best local artists are given exhibitions, like John Taylor, whose talent and singleminded devotion to his own sense of painter's truth, whatever the current fashion may dictate, together give rise to work that deserves to be known far beyond his native Glasgow.

PROJECT ABILITY, THIRD EYE CENTRE, 1983

As its name suggests, Project Ability is an organisation aimed at helping people with disabilities to fulfil innate creativity by all possible means. Project Ability was initiated by Third Eye Centre and the Scottish Committee on Arts and Disability in 1982 as a year-long project, with an October showcase season of exhibitions and events throughout Glasgow. Project Ability is now an independent educational charity.

KATE THOMSON, ARTIST IN RESIDENCE, THE ADELPHI NURSERY SCHOOL, 1987

Sculptor and community artist Kate Thomson, artist-in-residence, Gorbals Fair Society, and Gorbals youngsters turn a blank wall into a painted fantasy of colour and imagery. The mural, "The Four Seasons", is being painted in the Adelphi Nursery School. Glasgow, up till now, has enjoyed a reputation for racial harmony, something which must surely be encouraged by activities like this in a multi-racial district like Gorbals.

DEGREE SHOW, SCULPTURE SCHOOL, GLASGOW SCHOOL OF ART, 1987

The annual graduate show marks the first public appearance by would-be professional artists, some of whom will go on to success in their chosen career. This is a typical display of graduate students' work in the light and lofty sculpture studios in C. R. Mackintosh's famous building in Renfrew Street. One of the best art schools in the UK, GSA is back in the news with a batch of ambitious alumni who have found themselves in tune with the current fashion for figurative narrative painting on a mural scale. Students of sculpture, too, are returning to life-size figuration as seen here in an amusing contrast with the human element in the studio.

POLLOK HOUSE, POLLOK PARK, 1986

The 18th-century mansion of the Maxwells of Pollok, a family with a history that dates from the 12th century, has been attributed to William Adam, but the original house was extended with great sensitivity by the architect Sir Rowland Anderson when the late Sir John Stirling-Maxwell was the incumbent. Pollok House, with its furnishings and its fine collection of paintings and *objets d'art*, now belongs to the city within whose boundaries it lies — a remarkable oasis of *rus in urbe*, complete with lake, woodlands and a herd of highland cattle on the home farm.

PEOPLE'S PALACE, GLASGOW GREEN, 1986

The People's Palace on Glasgow Green (an extensive riverside acreage of common grassland which remains much as it was in the 18th century) is Glasgow's museum of social history and, as such, is highly popular with visitors and locals alike. It is here that you will find recorded and enthusiastically displayed in visual terms the story of the city's past, in trades, crafts, politics, sport, commerce — a township that grew from tiny mediaeval beginnings to industrial greatness in the 19th century; a city, indeed, that even in present times of great change, continues in the role of Scotland's greatest powerhouse of energy, creative and otherwise.

FOYER, JIMMY LOGAN'S METROPOLE THEATRE, 1965

This was the second Glasgow theatre of that name. Formerly the Empress Theatre, the building was saved by the actor/comedian Jimmy Logan and renamed the Metropole after the theatre in Stockwell Street in which Logan grew up as a junior member of a famous family of Glasgow entertainers, and which had been destroyed by fire in the early 1960s. It was in the new Metropole at St George's Cross that Scots comedy flourished for a number of years thereafter, without public subsidy and through Jimmy Logan's personal generosity.

CLYDE FAIR AT THE OLD FRUITMARKET, 1973

Enjoyable but abortive, Clyde Fair was the first attempt by Glaswegians to establish a spring festival of the arts — something that eventually came to pass with the founding of Mayfest, in 1982. Clyde Fair took place in 1973 and some of the most popular venues — with juveniles and adults alike — was the old Fruitmarket, virtually a street under cover, which had been left empty since the market's removal to new premises further east. Here were exhibitions, entertainers, rock and jazz bands, bars and restaurants: the essence was informality and Glasgow flocked to Candleriggs to enjoy itself.

CLYDE FAIR AT THE OLD FRUITMARKET, 1973

In this photograph something of the nostalgic quality of the old Fruitmarket may be seen: the floor of granite setts, the great spandrel window at the far end (rooflights, too, gave a spread of daylight over the whole area) and the remains of elegant gilt lettering above the stalls. But the children, eager to see what was happening inside the booths, had no interest in such mundane matters.

PAVEMENT ARTIST, SAUCHIEHALL STREET, 1984

The paving-over of city streets to make pedestrian precincts, plus the security offered by the daytime banning of motor vehicles, has given rise to a new breed of pavement artists, working on a large scale in exercising their craft — for it is very seldom art, as such, being mostly sedulous copying of postcard reproductions of famous masterpieces. Art or not, passers-by love to watch the work in progress.

MAYFEST, GEORGE SQUARE, 1986

"Mayfest Welcomes You To Glasgow" is the slogan blazoned throughout the city from the first day of May each year. It is a festival of the popular arts, growing in strength each year, which brings to Glasgow theatre groups, entertainers and artists from countries worldwide as well as from other parts of Britain. No rivalry with Edinburgh Festival is intended, Mayfest being not only less pretentious, and with a strong community emphasis, but also run on a small budget by comparison.

PENNY GEGGIES, BUCHANAN STREET, 1982

Pedestrian precincts offer a stage for street entertainers, the natural heirs of the buskers of old, no less professional, but usually drawn from a younger generation with boundless creative energy and the will to perform in public in the knowledge that financial rewards may well be microscopic. "Penny Geggies", initiated by Third Eye Centre, was the city's first festival of street entertainment. The venue, here, is Buchanan Street, the finest shopping precinct in Glasgow.

EDWIN MORGAN, "SONNETS FROM SCOTLAND" BOOKSIGNING, THIRD EYE CENTRE, 1986

Edwin Morgan is Glasgow's premier poet and highly respected man of letters; renowned, too, as one of the wittiest of Britain's concrete poets.

BILL FORSYTH AND CLARE GROGAN DURING THE FILMING OF "COMFORT AND JOY",
GLASGOW, 1983

With films based on his own Glasgow childhood, Bill Forsyth first made his name as an artist using cinema as his medium with *That Sinking Feeling*. The more ambitious *Comfort and Joy*, with Bill Paterson and Clare Grogan in the cast, brought him wide respect and critical acclaim. But Oscar Marzaroli's snap of Forsyth with Clare Grogan during filming in 1983 does exude a cheerful lack of pretension that is entirely typical of the man.

"SUGAR 'N' SPITE", LIZ LOCHHEAD, SIOBHAN REDMOND, ESTHER ALLAN, TRON THEATRE, 1982

It is some years since Glasgow's most accomplished poet-performer found an outlet in her gift for satirising human frailty and shortcomings from a female point of view. She is seen here in conjunction with the clever comic actress Siobhan Redmond, accompanied on the piano by Esther Allan.

MARCELLA EVARISTI AND ELAINE COLLINS, "TERRESTRIAL EXTRAS",
TRON THEATRE, MAYFEST 1986

The Tron Theatre, established in 1982 by Glasgow Theatre Club in a handsome and historic, disused church building near Glasgow Cross, is the city's home of studio theatre productions and shows like "Terrestrial Extras" in which actresses Marcella Evaristi and Elaine Collins impersonate a pair of visitors from outer space in order to make feminist, political and simply downright humorous capital.

"THE STEAMIE" AT GOVAN STEAMIE, WILDCAT STAGE PRODUCTIONS, MAYFEST 1987

The runaway theatrical success of Glasgow's Mayfest 1987 was the production, by Wildcat Stage Productions, of Tony Roper's play, "The Steamie", a nostalgic comedy about Glasgow's communal wash-houses (the photograph was taken at a performance in the now disused Govan steamie) in which a group of experienced comic players — Ida Schuster, Ray Jeffries, Elaine Smith, Katy Murphy and Dorothy Paul — recalled the days when the steamies were virtually the social clubs of Glasgow's working-class women.

DANCERS OF THE CELTIC BALLET, 1961

The Celtic Ballet was the brainchild of Margaret Morris who brought her progressive ideas about dance and the visual arts to Glasgow when she and her husband, J. D. Fergusson, left the south of France to settle in the city at the start of World War Two. Productions like "The Forsaken Mermaid", "The Earthshapers", "The Ballet of the Palette", brought together a number of avant garde talents, Morris herself as choreographer, Erik Chisholm as composer, the painters Josef Herman and William Crosbie in stage design.

GLASGOW THEATRE BALLET, REHEARSAL STUDIOS, 1968

After the demise of the Celtic Ballet in 1961 and before the foundation of Scottish Theatre Ballet (later Scottish Ballet) eight years later, dance lovers in the city looked to Glasgow Theatre Ballet for continuity. Like the Celtic Ballet this was a non-professional group, based on the Catherine Wells ballet school in the city's West End. But the work done was vitally important in training young dancers and in keeping interest in ballet alive.

"ROMEO AND JULIET", SCOTTISH BALLET, THEATRE ROYAL, 1982

In 1969, Peter Darrell, director of the touring dance company Western Theatre Ballet, was invited to bring his company to Glasgow to share Scottish Opera's newly acquired headquarters and rehearsal space in Elmbank Crescent, and to form the nucleus of a national ballet company. Scottish Ballet, now internationally known and respected, is a medium-size company geared to perform the classics (usually intelligently re-thought) and new full-length ballets as well as to create and encourage studio-scale contemporary dance works for touring, countrywide. "Romeo and Juliet", a revival of John Cranko's ballet to the music of Prokofiev, is one of Scottish Ballet's most ambitious productions. Elaine MacDonald, the company's prima ballerina, is seen in the photograph, partnered by Davide Bombana, at the Capulet's ball where Romeo and Juliet have their first meeting.

"L'EGISTO", SCOTTISH OPERA, THEATRE ROYAL, 1982

The development of Scottish Opera since its creation 25 years ago is one of the great success stories in a city where music has always been an important part of life. Not just the popular favourites — the 19th-century grand operas by Verdi, Wagner, Puccini and the rest — but rare items, too, like "L'Egisto" by the 17th-century composer Pier Francesco Cavalli, find a willing audience at Scottish Opera Theatre Royal — not least when the scene, by Allan Charles Klein, is made as decorative as this.

SIR ALEXANDER GIBSON, "LAST NIGHT AT THE PROMS"M, KELVIN HALL, 1982

By tradition, musical high jinks are not only allowed but even encouraged on the last night of the Proms. In this photograph, taken in 1982, Sir Alexander Gibson, conductor of the Scottish National Orchestra, looks on in benevolent amusement (baton still in operation, of course) as Donald Maxwell and Linda Ormiston perform a favourite party piece, the final quartette in Verdi's "Rigoletto" transformed, by dint of vocal and histrionic agility, into a duet.

CANTILENA, HENRY WOOD HALL, 1985

Cantilena is a remarkable chamber ensemble drawn from the Scottish National Orchestra, founded and directed by principal cellist Adrian Shepherd. Cantilena's reputation was swiftly made as a group capable of recharging baroque music for modern sensibilities through the use of modern instruments. The Henry Wood Hall is the Glasgow headquarters and rehearsal room of the SNO, converted from a substantial West End church.

ALLY BAIN IN CONCERT AT BABBITY BOWSTER, 1986

The development, and refurbishment for residential use, of the old merchant city of Glasgow between the mediaeval cathedral and the City Chambers in George Square has led to a resurgence of nightlife in a district which formerly found itself deserted when the working day was over. Babbity Bowster, a gracious little Adam townhouse in Blackfriars Street, now a bar, restaurant and hotel, has become a popular venue for informal evening entertainments, like this concert by Shetland fiddler Ally Bain.

CEILIDH WITH THE GALLIVANTERS AT THE WINTER GARDEN, PEOPLE'S PALACE, MAYFEST, 1987

The Winter Garden, adjoining the People's Palace, the great Victorian glasshouse which is bigger in area than the museum itself, has come triumphantly back into use as a popular venue for entertainments like the Mayfest Ceilidhs, organised by Third Eye Centre. The performers are The Gallivanters, playing traditional music to an appreciative audience.

In the TSWA 3D nationwide competition, a number of sites were specified and artists invited to submit ideas for related artworks. One of the winners, sculptor George Wyllie, created a straw locomotive to hang from the giant crane at Finnieston, a site selected by Third Eye Centre, the local organiser. The crane, in the great days of North British, "Locomotive Builders to the World", would be used to load real railway engines on to ships bound for distant countries.

The amazingly realistic structure of wire and straw was built full size and, hanging from the Finnieston crane during Mayfest 1987, it brought a lump to the throats of all those who remembered the days before the demise of the industry which Wyllie's work commemorated.

Page 195

NEW GLASGOW

Vast monumental city halls line the central squares of many British cities, relics and reminders of past grandeurs, and Glasgow is no exception. Its Town Council, which had met from time immemorial at the Cross of Glasgow, moved first to Wilson Street in 1842, then to Ingram Street in 1874 and finally to the present grandiose Municipal Buildings in George Square in 1889. With its face-lifting stone-cleaning it certainly presents no backward-looking image, and its proud banner underlines that corporate sentiment which no one, resident or visitor, would deny — "Glasgow Welcomes".

Gardner's warehouse in Jamaica Street, with its remarkable 1856 innovative alliance of glass with wrought and cast iron, is miraculously still here for us to marvel at. Other things, however, suffer change and decay, and the logo on the bus reminds us that what used to be the Town Council, became the Corporation and is now the District Council, no longer runs the once-familiar green and yellow trams, trolleys and buses through its own streets.

Glasgow's mosque, 1984, glistening like an Oriental gem-stone, affords an interesting contrast to the Criminal Court House fronting the south bank of the Clyde whose austere facade belies the surprising delicacy and architectural imagination of its interior.

The old Unitarian Church (1854) in St Vincent Street waits forlornly for its end before the onslaught of the tower-cranes busy with the new Britoil building.

Once the entrance to the St Enoch Underground Station, this bijou building is now a Travel Centre for the city's transport services. Built in 1896, it is a splendid and unexpected toy-like revival of the Jacobean style, spared for our enjoyment, while its neighbouring megalith, St Enoch Railway Station, has vanished without a trace.

One of the many unsolved mysteries of modern life is the actual purpose behind the bizarre proliferation of twinning cities. Is it done by drawing lots, or is there an International Twin City Allocation Council (ITCAC) which distributes these favours? Even more puzzling is how is it expected to enrich the lifestyle of, let's say, the entirely fictitious Mrs Sadie McGuffie, Flat 3/4, Block E, The Gorbals?

It has been said that when Charles Rennie Mackintosh designed a house, he insisted on designing everything from the ashtrays to the chimney pots. This range included an idiosyncratic lettering style, with double-barred "H"s, groups of repetitious little squares, and so on. Not a particularly felicitous alphabet, it has nevertheless been seized upon by the fashion-conscious. It is to be hoped that its debased appearance on a shop fascia heralds its end, but we should be so lucky!

The People's Palace was built in 1898 with £18,000 compensation from the Caledonian Railway Company for permission to run a railway line under Glasgow Green. It combined an art gallery, a museum, recreation and reading rooms and a winter garden. The latter lay for long unused and under threat, but persistent and energetic activity by the museum staff and by the Friends of the People's Palace have gained it a respite. It now provides an airy ambience where the beating mind can be stilled midst graceful foliage, sweet birdsong, and the company of Smudge the Palace Cat!

In the photograph of Trinity, College Towers from the Scottish Exhibition and Conference Centre, the placing of every object, every patch of dark and light, every contrast between organic and inorganic, make an essential contribution, but underlying it is still the unstructured reality of the actual world — the towers of Park Church (1858) now a preserved sham and the three Lombardic towers of Trinity College (1862) on the heights of Park Circus.

The fact that Templeton's carpet factory facade was based on the Doge's Palace in Venice is fairly well known, but the sight of this bizarre and totally unexpected building on the north side of Glasgow Green is still capable of giving a visual shock. Designed by the Glasgow architect William Leiper, and built in 1899, its oddity has been popularly explained as exasperation on the patron's part over the architect's inability to produce an acceptable original design — another urban myth! The polychrome tiles and the faintly bauhaus-style windows attract most attention, but the elaborate brickwork is every bit as exciting. No longer a thriving carpet factory it is now part of a £3 million industrial estate.

It might be supposed that Glasgow children — a totally urban race for whom grass and trees grow in District Council parks and for whom milk comes in cans or bottles — are essentially deprived and underprivileged. The delights of the urban playground, the interconnected back courts and closes for hide-and-seek, the smooth level surface for peerie spinning and kick-the-can, the low garden walls for high tig, the broad pavements for running geggies and bogies along — these are the city delights that the rural child, poor soul that he is, knows nothing of!